iCan iPod

MENU

Shelley O'Hara

que®

800 East 96th Street,
Indianapolis, Indiana 46240 USA

iCan iPod

International Standard Book Number: 0-7897-3527-X

Library of Congress Catalog Card Number: 2005932885

Printed in the United States of America

First Printing: November 2005

09 08 07 06 05 4 3 2 1

Trademarks

All terms mentioned in this book that are known to be trademarks or service marks have been appropriately capitalized. Que Publishing cannot attest to the accuracy of this information. Use of a term in this book should not be regarded as affecting the validity of any trademark or service mark.

Warning and Disclaimer

Every effort has been made to make this book as complete and as accurate as possible, but no warranty or fitness is implied. The information provided is on an "as is" basis. The author and the publisher shall have neither liability nor responsibility to any person or entity with respect to any loss or damages arising from the information contained in this book.

Bulk Sales

Que Publishing offers excellent discounts on this book when ordered in quantity for bulk purchases or special sales. For more information, please contact

U.S. Corporate and Government Sales
1-800-382-3419
corpsales@pearsontechgroup.com

For sales outside of the U.S., please contact

International Sales
international@pearsoned.com

Associate Publisher
Greg Wiegand

Acquisitions Editor
Stephanie J. McComb

Development Editor
Laura Norman

Managing Editor
Charlotte Clapp

Project Editor
Mandie Frank

Production Editor
Heather Wilkins

Proofreader
Lisa Wilson

Publishing Coordinator
Sharry Lee Gregory

Interior Designer
Anne Jones

Cover Designer
Greg Yurchuk

Page Layout
Brad Chinn

Contents at a Glance

Table of Contents

About the Author

Shelley O'Hara is the author of more than 100 books, including several of the best-selling *Easy Windows* books. She also teaches at the Indianapolis campus of Indiana and Purdue Universities. Her son let her borrow his U2 iPod (grudgingly) to work on this book.

Dedication

Dedicated to my son Michael O'Hara and his two best friends, John Van Winkle and Andrew Hilger; all three iPod, music, and film aficionados.

Acknowledgments

I'm grateful to Stephanie McComb who got me involved in this project; I'm lucky to work with her on this and many other projects. Sharry Lee Gregory not only keeps the paper-work flowing, she makes the process personal and fun. Mille grazie (a million thanks). The insightful comments of Laura Norman made this a better book, as did the careful editing by Mandie Frank and Heather Wilkins.

Photo Credits

All product photos used on the cover and in the book are owned by the respective manufacturers, including but not limited to DesignerSkins; Apple; Sony; Altec-Lansing; DLO/Netalog; Griffin Technology; Monster Cable Products; iSkin; iPoDonut; Hewlett-Packard; Speck; RadTech; Acme; Becky's Beads; Think Different Store; Crystal Icing; MacMedia, Inc.; Alscher; GioFX; XtremeMac; Belkin; and SDI Technologies Hasbro.

We Want to Hear from You!

As the reader of this book, *you* are our most important critic and commentator. We value your opinion and want to know what we're doing right, what we could do better, what areas you'd like to see us publish in, and any other words of wisdom you're willing to pass our way.

As an Associate Publisher for Que Publishing, I welcome your comments. You can email or write me directly to let me know what you did or didn't like about this book—as well as what we can do to make our books better.

Please note that I cannot help you with technical problems related to the topic of this book. We do have a User Services group, however, where I will forward specific technical questions related to the book.

When you write, please be sure to include this book's title and author as well as your name, email address, and phone number. I will carefully review your comments and share them with the author and editors who worked on the book.

Email: feedback@quepublishing.com

Mail: Greg Wiegand
Associate Publisher
Que Publishing
800 East 96th Street
Indianapolis, IN 46240 USA

For more information about this book or another Que Publishing title, visit our website at www.quepublishing.com. Type the ISBN (excluding hyphens) or the title of a book in the Search field to find the page you're looking for.

Introduction

Why should you get a book about what you can do with your iPod? First, you probably don't know everything about what you can do although you probably *think* you do. New gadgets and mini-programs are introduced all the time. Second, when you discover something new and cool, you can share it with your friends, making you the iPodMaster. Third, if your parents are hesitant to let you get an iPod, you can convince them by maturely explaining some of the educational stuff available. And finally, you can have *even* more fun!

As a little preview of what's covered in this book, see whether you know the following:

Questions	Knew That	New to Me
Did you know there's a new iPod model available now called the nano?	❑	❑
Did you know that all new iPod models come with color displays?	❑	❑
Did you know that you can display 25,000 photos on your iPod?	❑	❑
Did you know that you can listen to books on your iPod?	❑	❑
Did you know that you can use the iGuy, a bendable little guy that holds your iPod and sits in a dock to recharge your iPod?	❑	❑
Did you know you can get a pink crocodile flip purse for your iPod mini?	❑	❑
Did you know that you can print tattoos to customizethe look of your iPod?	❑	❑

Questions	Knew That	New to Me
Did you know that you can have your music collection available from a portable player for parties?	❑	❑
Did you know that you can listen to your iPod through a car stereo system or your home stereo system?	❑	❑
Did you know that you can get a clock/radio alarm that wakes you up to iPod music? And lets you fall asleep to music (turning off the iPod automatically)?	❑	❑
Did you know that you can display lyrics and sing along to your favorite tune on your iPod?	❑	❑
Did you know that you can record your singing or other sounds or thoughts?	❑	❑

Yep, you can do all this and more! This book expands the already cool iPod possibilities. So read on, experiment, and have fun.

Chapter 1

Do You iPod?

If you are reading this book, you probably already own an iPod, are thinking of buying one yourself, or are hoping that someone buys one for you. (Isn't your birthday coming up?) There are four models of Apple iPods: the regular or classic iPod, the iPod mini, the iPod nano, and the iPod shuffle. Which one do you have? Which one do you *wish* you had? Do you even know how they are different?

In this chapter we'll talk about all four models of iPods and you'll have answers to these questions:

- How are the models of iPods different?
- What features does my iPod have?
- How can I find accessories that work with my iPod model?

What's the Difference?

The various iPod models are different in these important ways:

- **Price**—It's not surprising that one of the main differences is the price. And like gaming systems, skateboards, and just about every other thing, the fancier the iPod, the more you pay. You can expect to pay from $99 for the iPod shuffle to $429 for the customized U2 version of the classic iPod. If you are shopping for a new iPod, price might be the determining factor in which one you get. What do you get for the money? More music and more features. Read on to find out what more money buys you.

Tip

If you want to save money, consider purchasing an older model iPod. You can find these for sale online at places such as eBay, buy.com, and others. You might be able to get a discount on current models online, too. If you shop at Apple or other retail stores, the prices will be more consistent and probably a little higher than online.

- **Storage space or how many songs it can hold**—Like your computer's hard drive, iPod has its own storage device and its size is measured in megabytes (MB) or gigabytes (GB). The storage space varies depending on the model. In addition to this gigabyte measurement, Apple also provides an estimate of the number of songs you can store, and this is likely what's important to you. Sizes range from 512MB or 120 songs (the smallest iPod shuffle) to 60GB or 15,000 songs (the classic iPod). Read the fine print when thinking about these song estimates: The number of songs is based on certain standards such as the song length (4 minutes) and the type of music file, so your actual results may be different.

- **Physical size**—In addition to the storage size, the physical size (weight and measurements) of the iPod models vary. The smallest weighs about as much as your house key and is smaller than a candy bar; the largest weighs 6 ounces or a little less than one half of a pound (think about the weight of two quarter-pound hamburgers) and is about the size of a deck of cards.
- **Charge time and battery life**—Your iPod runs on a rechargeable battery, and your *battery life* determines how long you can use your iPod until you need to recharge the battery. If you are going on a long trip, the battery life is important. You don't want to run out of music halfway across the Nevada desert. The iPod shuffle has a battery life of 12 hours compared to 18 hours for the iPod mini. The

charge time is the time it takes to completely recharge your iPod; expect 4 hours on the iPod shuffle and iPod mini and 5 hours for the classic iPod.

- **Display size**—The iPod mini and classic iPod have little display screens where you can select commands and view information such as the song title. The iPod mini has a smaller display than the classic iPod (makes sense since the whole thing is smaller); it also displays only in black, white, and shades of gray. The newest generation classic iPod has a two-inch color display. The iPod shuffle does not include a display.
- **Features**—All four iPod models have different features. You can customize some iPods, but not others. You can view photos, for instance, on some, but not all. For more info, read about what features are included with each model in the following detailed sections.

Tip

Apple has introduced new versions of the classic iPod, and you'll hear and see these referred to as generations—for instance, 1G, 2G, 3G, and 4G. (Don't confuse that with the storage size!) Also, some add-ons or accessories might work with only a specific generation. If you are unsure whether an add-on or accessory will work with

your iPod, email or call the seller and get more information.

When you get ready to buy something or are comparing models, you usually focus on what's different. It's important to know that iPods do share several common features, including

- All iPods work with either a Macintosh or Windows-based computer; they also include the right software for hooking up with iTunes, Apple's player and music management program.
- All iPods include a USB port for connecting your iPod to your computer. For the iPod mini and classic iPod, the cable is included. For the iPod shuffle, you need to purchase a USB cable. You can also use a FireWire connection or a docking device, depending on the iPod model and whether your computer has a FireWire port.
- All iPods include headphones and provide skip protection so you can listen to your iPod while jogging or walking your rowdy dog, Louie.
- You can purchase accessories that work with your iPod; you'll learn more about accessories—docks, headphones, holders, and so on—later in this book.

Now that you have some idea of what makes each iPod model different (as well as what they share in common), let's take a look at each model in more detail.

The iPod Shuffle

Ask yourself the following questions to see whether the iPod shuffle is a good match for you and your musical style:

- Do you want the smallest iPod, one you can carry in your pocket?
- Do you want the least expensive iPod?
- Do you want the simplest iPod?
- Do you like surprises when you listen to your music?

If you answered "yes" to these questions, consider the iPod shuffle. Weighing in at less an ounce (.78 ounce), this player weighs about the same as your house key and is a little more than 3 inches long; it's the smallest of all iPod players (see Figure 1.1). The iPod shuffle also is the simplest to use and the least expensive ($99 for the 512MB player).

The iPod shuffle comes with a storage capacity of 512MB (120 songs) or 1GB (240 songs), and it has a battery life of roughly 12 hours. After you add songs to the player, iPod shuffle plays them back in a random order (hence the name *shuffle*).

Figure 1.1

Of the different iPods, the iPod shuffle is the smallest in physical size and storage capacity.

Because songs are played randomly, you don't need a display, but the player does include buttons for playing, pausing, skipping to the next song, replaying a song, and stopping play. If you aren't in the mood for a particular song when it plays, skip to the next. Want to play a song again? Repeat the song.

Caution

The iPod shuffle does not include a USB cable for connecting your iPod to your computer. You need to purchase this separately.

The Table 1.1 provides the details of the iPod shuffle at a glance.

Table 1.1 The iPod Shuffle

Storage	512MB (120 songs) or 1GB (240 songs)
Display	None
Battery life	12 hours
Charge time	4 hours
Size	3.3″ × .98″ × .33″
Weight	.78 ounce
Connection	USB 1.1 through 2.0, cable not included

The iPod Mini

One step up on the iPod ladder you'll find the iPod mini. This model is a good mix of affordability and features. It's more expensive than the iPod shuffle, but less expensive than the iPod. It includes more features than the iPod shuffle, but less than the iPod. It's larger than the iPod shuffle, but smaller than the iPod.

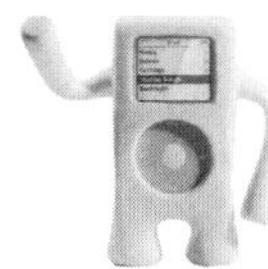

Tip

One cool thing about the iPod mini is that it comes in several neat colors. You can choose from a metallic silver, pink, green, or blue.

It weighs 3.6 ounces (that's a little less than a bar of soap and less than one-fourth the weight of the full size model), and it's slightly longer than the iPod shuffle (3.6″ long versus 3.3″). The width is 2 inches, making room for a small grayscale display (see Figure 1.2).

Figure 1.2

The iPod mini includes a display and a click wheel for selecting songs and adjusting the volume.

For a quick summary of the iPod mini specs, check out Table 1.2.

Table 1.2 The iPod Mini

Storage	4GB (1,000 songs) or 6GB (1,500 songs)
Display	1.67″ grayscale
Battery life	18 hours
Charge time	4 hours
Size	3.6″ × 2″ × .5″
Weight	3.6 ounces
Connection	USB 2.0 and FireWire (FireWire cable not included)

Note

In September of 2005, Apple introduced the Apple nano, a replacement for the iPod mini. You can read about this new product later in the chapter. You can still find minis for sale at sites that offer older models of the iPod, and the mini was Apple's most popular product, so many of y'all might already have a mini.

The Classic iPod

Quiz time again. To see whether the classic iPod is the perfect match for you, consider these questions:

- Do you have enough money to pay for the full-size iPod? Price is usually the deciding factor in what iPod you get.
- Do you want to be able to store as many tunes as possible?
- Do you want to have the most control over playing songs, adding cool stuff, and customizing your iPod?

Then put all your money down on a classic iPod. Although this model is the most expensive, it also offers the most storage space, most features, and a color display (newest models). While it's bigger than its brother players, the size is manageable. You can fit it into your pocket or purse.

Besides price, the key difference is the iPod's storage capacity: You can store up to 20GB (5,000 songs) or 60GB (15,000 songs) depending on which version you have. (An older generation model is also available with a 30GB storage capacity.) With the ability to store that many songs, you can most likely include your entire music library on one little portable device. You don't need to lug around your fat CD album or wallet; you simply need your iPod and your earphones.

At 4.1" in length and 2.4" wide, the iPod is about the size of a deck of cards. At the top of the player, you see the display, and beneath that, you can find the click wheel (see Figure 1.3). On the newest iPods, the 2-inch display can display 65,000+ colors.

Figure 1.3

You can view the menu in the display; use the click wheel to scroll through menu selections.

Like the iPod mini, you can store files, schedule alarms, store your friends' contact info, and play games. The classic iPod also includes these features:

- In addition to files, you can store and display pictures on your iPod (20,000 to 25,000 photos). Chapter 11 covers some of the cool photo options including sharing and viewing photos.

Note

A word on color. iPod used to offer an iPod Photo that you could use to display pictures. That model is no longer available because now all new iPods and iPod nanos include color displays, and you can store and display pictures on these models.

- Use the customized menu to create on-the-go playlists, rate songs, select the language, control equalizer settings, and more.
- Connect your iPod to your TV or projector through the audio-video (AV) port and display slideshows with your music. The AV cable for this connection is not included.

Table 1.3 lists the important details about the iPod.

Table 1.3 The Classic iPod

Storage	20GB (5,000 songs) or 60GB (15,000 songs)
Display	2″ 65,356 color display
Battery life	15 hours (5 hours for slideshows with music)
Charge time	5 hours
Size	4.1″ × 2.4″ × .75″
Weight	5.9 or 6.4 ounces
Connection	USB 2.0, FireWire, AV ports. (FireWire and AV cable sold separately.) AC adapter.

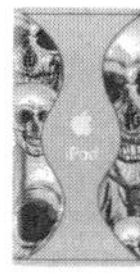

Caution

This chapter focused on the current iPod generations (fourth generation). If you have an earlier generation, you might notice some differences. You can read more about the differences in generations online at sites such as the Canadian user site, www.ehmac.ca/archive/index.php/t-22431.html.

Can You Say Nano?

In September 2005, Apple introduced a new iPod called nano (see Figure 1.4). This model replaces the iPod mini and offers several enhancements over the mini, including the following:

Figure 1.4

Check out the new iPod nano, a replacement for the iPod mini.

- The size is smaller and more compact; the nano weighs less than a CD and is skinnier than a pencil!
- A color display lets you check out album art in color as you listen to songs. Like other color iPods, you can also display 25,000 photos on your iPod. (Photos are covered in Chapter 11.)
- You can pick from two storage capacities: the 4G nano holds about 1,000 songs and costs $249, and the 2G nano holds about 500 songs and costs $199.
- You can do all the things on the nano that you could with the mini: play games, read audio books, add notes and contact information, and so on. If you do get a nano, the information in this book will still help you learn all the cool things you can do with it.

Right now only a few accessories are available, and they are similar to those available for the iPod mini and classic iPod. You can purchase headphones such as a lanyard style headphone that you wear around your neck, a power adapter for charging the nano, a dock that enables you to connect your iPod nano to home or car stereos as well as your PC, an arm band for running or riding bikes, and tubes to add some flair and protection to your iPod. Check out Apple's website (www.apple.com/ipodnano/) to see the details of this new iPod as well as see the available accessories. (Expect also for other companies to create and market accessories for this new iPod very soon.)

Coming Attractions...

To listen to music you need earphones, and although all of the iPods come with earphones, you might decide to upgrade to a different type of earphone. Or perhaps you want to be able to listen to your iPod without earphones, using a boombox, for instance. The next chapter covers the different accessories for listening to your iPod.

Chapter 2

Listen Up: iPod Audio Gear

All iPods come with earbud-style headphones (small speakers that fit into the ear), and these might suit you just fine. On the other hand, you might prefer a different type of headphone. You might like street style, or perhaps you want some heavy-duty headphones that filter out background noise. There are lots of reasons to change to a different type of headphone—for more comfort, a different look, or for better-quality sound. The first part of this chapter gives you all the headphone choices available.

After you are listening in style, you might want to share the love. Why shouldn't your friends be able to listen to your musical collection? They can. You can add speakers to your iPod, replacing your stereo system with an iPod. After all, the iPod stores your entire music collection. You can also buy an iPod-ready boombox to hook your iPod to and let everyone in earshot rock to your music. Or, with the right adapter, you can hook up your iPod to your current stereo. Lots of choices. And for the utmost control, add a remote control so you can adjust the volume or change songs from across the room. The second part of this chapter covers all these listening choices.

Headphone Choices

The earbud headphones included with your iPod are a reasonable listening option. The speakers are small (like *buds*) and fit into your ears (sort of Secret Service style). The headphone cable connects to the player. You might, though, want a different type of headphone. Here are some reasons you might think about new headphones:

- Your mom always told you never to stick anything (except your elbow) into your ear, so you want headphones that fit around your ear instead of in your ear.
- The earbuds are uncomfortable. More padding, please? Or a different size?
- The cord is a drag, literally. You prefer a wireless solution to listening.
- The quality of regular headphones might be okay for amateurs, but you need the best quality sound with noise canceling and other top-notch qualities.
- You look cute in a headband and prefer a headphone style that sits on top of your head (or fits behind your ears).

- You lost your headphones and need a replacement pair. Or you like to have two sets of headphones, depending on your mood.

Regardless of the reason, you can find lots of headphone choices, ranging in price from $6.99 to $500. That's some serious cash for headphones. You'll need a big allowance or have to do lots of babysitting if you want the high-end headphones. Let's look at some of your choices.

Upgrading Your Headphones

If the style is your most important consideration or if you want something relatively inexpensive, you can explore some of the different headphone styles, including the following:

- Headband-style headphones have padded ear covers that sit on top of your ears. The headband may fit behind or over your head. Some have large padded ear covers, known as *street style* headphones (see Figure 2.1). You might choose these if you don't like having plugs in your ears. You can find inexpensive styles ranging in prices from $7 to $40 or more. Popular manufacturers include Sony and Colby.
- If you don't like how earbuds feel, you can purchase other styles of plugs, including Griffin's EarJams or CMO's Earbuds (with a

retractable cord). Some earplugs have hooks that fit over your ear to keep the plug in place (for example, the set made by Koss). Some are designed to stay in place if you are a runner (for example, Nike Flight Lightweight Sport Headphones). The price for these earphones range from $10 to $20 or more.

Figure 2.1

You can select a different headphone style than the earbuds included with your iPod.

In addition to different styles, you can find headphones that provide better sound quality. If you look at advertisements for these headphones, they all claim to "take your music to the next level," provide a "true audiophile experience," or give you "studio-quality sound." You might see technical specifications about the headphone on the packaging or in the product information. But who wants to become an expert on the lingo for headphones?

Instead, the best way to pick better quality headphones is to visit an electronics store and try them out. You should be able to hear a difference in the $20 version when compared to the $100 version or the $150+ version. If you don't, why bother upgrading? You can also go online and visit forums. Read reviews from real users to see what they have to say. You can also ask your friends what headphones they like and recommend.

If you upgrade for quality, you can plan on dropping some major cash. Sennheiser, for instance, offers noise-canceling headphones priced at $100 to $120 or more. Shure has quality earbud-style headphones priced at $100 and $180. Sony's run from $100 to $140. You can also find wireless headphones with a built-in wireless adapter; these run around $100 or more. Try Logitech Wireless Headphones for iPod, priced at $150, for instance. This wireless set works only with iPod and iPod mini (not iPod shuffle).

Adding an Extra Set of Ears to Your iPod

Although you might not want to share your iPod with your little brother, you might find that you don't mind sharing with that someone special. Music is more fun when it's shared!

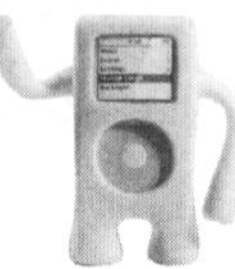

Tip

The cheap way of sharing is for each person to plug one earbud into one ear. This method keeps you very close, but it's hard to hear the music and get comfortable.

You can purchase a special add-on device, such as the Monster iSplitter, XtremeMac Audio Splitter, or other similar products so you can share the tunes. You can connect this to your iPod so you have plugs for two sets of headphones. Then you and a friend can listen at the same time. (Of course, someone will have to control which songs you listen to. *That's* still grounds for argument.)

You can purchase one of these splitters at online stores such as http://store.apple.com or www.everythingipod.com. They are also pretty inexpensive, around $12 to $15, well worth the price if you can make a new friend by sharing. Also, Target has a decent selection of iPod items. You can look there as well as try computer and electronic stores like Circuit City and Best Buy.

Play It Out Loud

Jamming by yourself in your own little music world with your headphones on is okay, but don't you wish your iPod could be your stereo? That you didn't have to wear headphones to enjoy the music? Then you'd have all of your music available at your fingertips. You could also play songs from your CD collection (loaded to your iPod) and songs you purchased online one right after the other. Wouldn't that be a dream come true?

Well, with a few accessories, you can do just that: Make your iPod into a stereo or boombox. You can connect your iPod to an existing stereo or purchase an iPod-ready speaker system or boombox player. This section covers the presto change-o magic of using your iPod as a stereo.

Just Add Speakers

If you want good quality sound in a totally sweet-looking design, you can find several speaker products that work with your iPod, including products from well-known companies such as Bose, Altec, and Klipsch. You simply connect your iPod to the stereo system, sit back, and enjoy the music (see Figure 2.2). These products work great in your bedroom, at your desk, or as a replacement for your home stereo system.

Figure 2.2

Connect your iPod to a speaker system and let everyone enjoy the music.

Like other products covered in this book, you'll find there's a wide price range, from $99 to $400 or more. What's the difference among the systems? Here's a quick look at iPod speaker system differences:

- **Sound quality**—The most important system feature to consider (along with price) is the sound quality. If you understand all the terms such as woofer, subwoofer, tweeter, and so on, you'll be able to compare sound systems with no help at all. On the other hand, if woofer and tweeter sound like names of cartoon characters, don't worry. Instead, visit an Apple store if you have one in your area or another electronic store such as Best Buy or Frys and listen to the various speaker systems. Let your ears decide. You can also read reviews written by actual users at http://www.everythingipod.com or Apple's online store, store.apple.com.

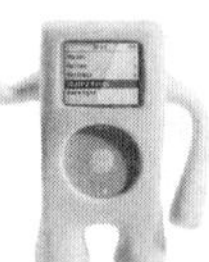

Tip

Each person expects something different from their stereo, and this can also be related to the type of music he enjoys. Michael, for instance, might be big on the bass. In this case, a system that has a quality bass sound would rank higher in his estimation. John, on the other hand, might prefer range. How loud he can crank the stereo and how far he can hear the music might be top on his evaluation list.

- **Size and portability**—Some systems are *portable*; you can move them from room to room. These systems might work perfect in your bedroom, but also can be taken to a party or other gathering. Other systems are larger and aren't designed to be moved from one place to another.

- **Connection**—As mentioned, you plug in your iPod and play your music, but how you plug it in varies. Some systems include a built-in dock, and you simply drop in your iPod. Others might require a docking station. When adding up the cost, be sure to figure in the cost of any extra accessories you need to set up the system, such as cables or special adapters.

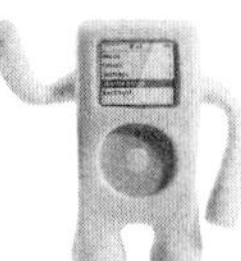

Tip

Some systems include plugs so you can connect other equipment (laptops, other iPods, CD players, MP3 players) to the speakers, too. If you have other music equipment you want to hook up, make sure your system has extra input jacks so you have enough spots to plug in everything.

- **iPod models**—Most systems work with the iPod and iPod mini, but only a few work with the iPod shuffle. When shopping, be sure you check to make sure the system works with the iPod model you have.
- **Remote**—Some systems come with a remote you can use to control the player from across the room. See the section "Controlling Tunes with a Remote" later in this chapter for more

information on remotes. Again, you can usually add a remote later, but you'll want to check the cost when comparing systems that might include a remote as part of the package.

- **Power**—Some systems work on batteries as well as electricity; some work only on electricity. If you want a system that you can take camping or take to a party without worrying about a power supply, get one that runs on batteries. If your iPod stereo will stay in the same spot, one that plugs into an electrical outlet is fine.

To give you an idea of some of the types of sound systems you can get and their price ranges, take a look at Table 2.1. This table doesn't include every single speaker system available and new products are introduced all the time, so use this list as a starting point in investigating which system works best for you.

Table 2.1 Popular Sound Systems

Product	Estimated Price
Creative TravelSound Travel Speakers	$89.95
Altec Lansing inMotion Portable Speakers	$129
JBL On Tour Portable Music Box	$159.95

Product	Estimated Price
JBL On Stage	$159.95
Altec Lansing IM3c	$179
Bose SoundDock Digital Music System	$299
Klipsch iFi	$399

Boom Baby! Your iPod As a Boombox

Although some of the speaker systems mentioned in the previous table are portable, you might like the look and style of the traditional boombox. When you add your iPod, your boombox can then play anything in your entire music collection. You can take your boombox to the beach, a friend's house, a party, a dance, or wherever you can liven things up with your music (see Figure 2.3).

The first boombox and a popular model is the DLO iBoom Boombox (priced at $129.99). This system includes FM radio and is powered by batteries or AC power (you plug it into an electrical outlet). To help you cart your boombox around, you can also purchase an optional carrying case (priced at $44.99).

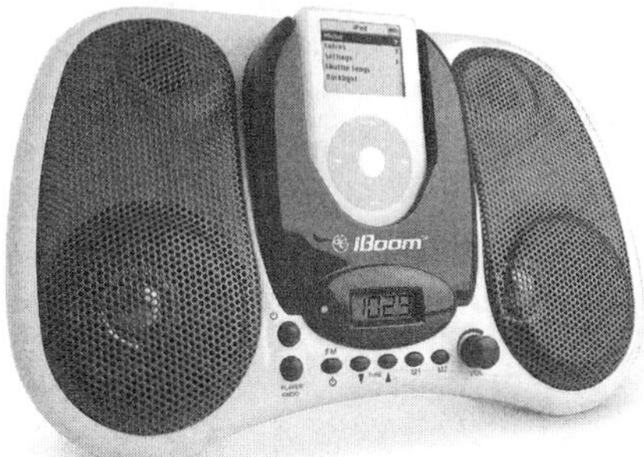

Figure 2.3

For portable music with your iPod, consider a boombox—too cool!

Connecting Your Stereo To Your iPod

If you already have a kickin' stereo, you don't need to purchase yet another system for your iPod. In many cases, you can connect your iPod to your existing stereo system. All you need is a stereo connection kit such as Apple iPod Stereo Connection Kit with Monster Cable (priced at $79). This kit includes a docking station, power adapter, dock connecter to FireWire cable, and audio cable. You have to sort out what plugs in where, so read the directions.

Controlling Tunes with a Remote

If you do use a speaker system, your iPod has to sit in its little throne, connected to the speakers. You can't hold it in your hot little hands and control it. So that you don't have to exert any extra energy, you can get a remote. Then you can control the playback from across the room (or even in another room on another floor if you have a high-powered remote).

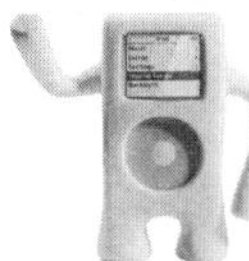

Tip

Your remote will also work if you have set up your iPod to play in your car. Chapter 3, "Take It with You: iPod Travel Accessories," covers car stereo options for your iPod. Even if you don't drive, your older brother or sister might have an iPod car system. Or perhaps your parents are ultra cool and even *they* have an iPod and car setup.

As mentioned, some systems come with remotes, but you can also purchase and use remotes with your iPod as long as it is hooked up to self-powered stereo speakers.

Most remotes do the following:

- Move to the next track or playlist.
- Play a previous track or playlist.
- Shuffle songs.
- Repeat a song.
- Adjust the volume.

One thing you can't do is scroll through your music collection and select a particular song, album, or artist using the remote. You start by selecting the artist, album, or playlist using the iPod; then you can scroll through those songs using the Next or Previous buttons.

Caution

Most of the speaker systems and remotes do not work with the iPod shuffle. If you have the iPod shuffle, check Apple's site to see specifically what accessories are available for this iPod.

If a remote is a must-have for you, you can find product information, pricing, and feature lists at sites that sell iPod gear, such as www.everythingipod.com and http://store.apple.com. Popular remotes include Ten Technology naviPro eX Wireless Remote Control ($49.95), DLO iDirect Remote Control for iPod ($39.99), and Griffin AirClick ($39.99).

Coming Attractions

In this chapter, you saw how you have choices about the ways you listen to your iPod. You can also take your iPod on the road by listening to it in the car, the topic of the next chapter. You'll also learn about handy carrying devices that make sure your iPod is always handy.

Chapter 3

Take It with You: iPod Travel Accessories

You aren't one to stay in one place very long, and your iPod is designed to go with you. Nothing can make a long car trip more fun than your companion iPod. To make traveling with your iPod easier, you can find a ton of accessories; you can broadcast your iPod through a FM car radio or attach your iPod to a handy arm band for running around or riding your bike. You can even find waterproof holders so you and your iPod can go on a synchronized swim. These and other travel options are the featured topic of this chapter.

Road Trip

Although you probably can't drive *yet*, you will still find yourself as a passenger in the car. Car pooling to school. Road trips to visit Grandma. The family vacation to the Grand Canyon. Of course, you could recline in the backseat in your own little world, soundtrack provided by your iPod. Or you could share the music.

Let's start by seeing what car stereo options are available for your iPod. Then you can find out about car chargers and holders for you and your traveling iPod.

iPod on the FM Dial

Rather than listen to the same old music on the radio stations or to boring disc jockeys, why not listen to your own music? Even if you have a CD player, it's a hassle to lug around your CDs, find the CD you want, and insert it into the player. Plus, with an iPod you can switch songs, artists, and music styles easily, and all your songs are available all the time. Try getting that same selection with a CD player, even one that holds multiple CDs.

To use your iPod in your car, you buy a car kit and then the music is broadcast through your FM radio. There are some of the drawbacks to this type of connection:

- To listen to your music, you need to find an open FM station. And if you are driving through different cities or states, you'll need to adjust the station to find a clear one in that area. Finding an open channel isn't always as simple as it sounds.
- Even with different open channels, the frequency can vary. And for the best sound quality, you need to find the strongest signal. This might require a little searching.
- Where you live might affect the strength of the signal. For instance, if you live in a big city, you might find it hard to get a strong enough signal for good quality sound.
- The sound quality through FM radio waves is not CD-quality sound. Also, static can be a problem on some stations.

Of the products available, each promises to deal with the preceding factors. That is, they promise to make it easy to find good, clear frequencies; change frequencies; and get high-quality sound. Don't believe everything they say.

The best way for you to pick a product is to check out online reviews. The Apple online site (http://store.apple.com), for instance, includes reviews from *actual* users for its products. So instead of marketing hype, you can read about real experiences with the product. Also, you might see if you can test "drive" the products to listen for yourself.

You can find several iPod FM transmitters on the market. Although Table 3.1 doesn't hit every single product available (new products are introduced all the time), you can get an idea of what's out there, who makes this type of accessory, and what the cost might be.

Table 3.1 iPod FM Transmitters

Product	Price
Griffin iTrip (see Figure 3.1)	$34.95
Griffin iTrip for iPod mini	$39.95
Monster iCarPlay Wireless Plus	$79.95
XtremeMac AirPlay FM Transmitter and XtremeMac AirPlay for iPod Shuffle	$39.95 or $49.95 for the iPod shuffle version
DLO TransPod All-In-One Car Solution	$79.99. Available for for iPod mini ($99.99) and iPod shuffle ($59.99) as well

Tip

Some car radio iPod accessories will also work with your home radio.

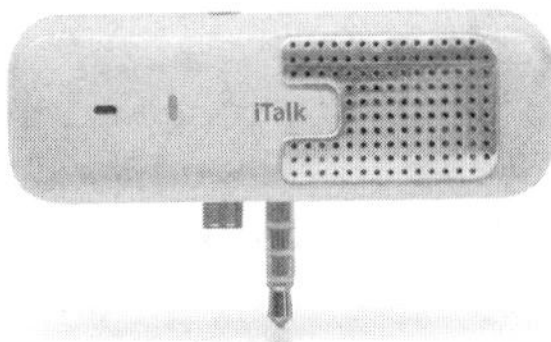

Figure 3.1

Play your iPod tunes through a car stereo with an iTrip.

A New Use for Your Cassette Player

If your car is ancient, it might include a cassette player, and while you probably lack a selection of cassettes to actually play in this dinosaur music player, you can use the car's cassette player to play your iPod. The cassette adapter kit is a cassette with a cable attached; you insert the cassette into the player and then connect the cable to your iPod's headphone jack. You can then play music through your car stereo system.

Cassette adapters are relatively inexpensive—from $20 to $40. If you are interested, check out Sony's CPA-9C Car Cassette Adapter, Monster iCarPlay Cassette Adapter (see Figure 3.2), DLO Direct Connect Kit Car Solution, or XtremeMac Audio Kit (works for iPod shuffle).

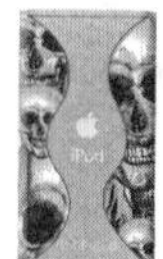

Caution

Check the return policy on these products. Current reviews cite some problems: the cassette keeps ejecting, the music skips, or the cassette flips from side A to side B. So if it doesn't work, you want to be sure you can return it for a refund (rather than getting yet another copy of the same product that won't work for your player).

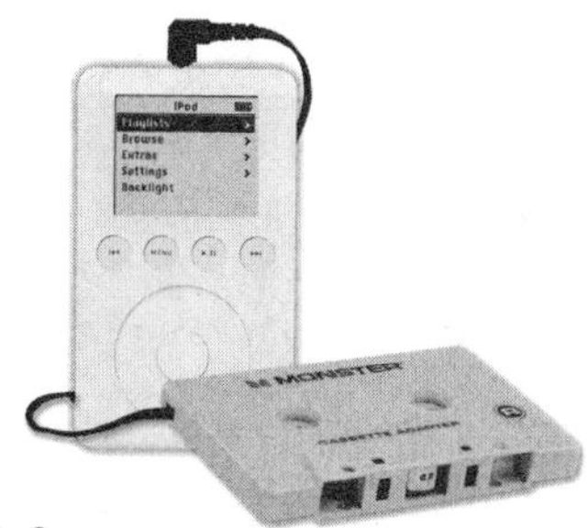

Figure 3.2

If your family car has a cassette player, you can get a cassette adapter to play your iPod through the car's stereo.

Charging Your iPod on the Road

One accessory that's useful for non-drivers and for those that don't care to share the music via the car stereo is a charger. If you are in for a long car ride, you don't want to run out of music halfway across Kansas. Instead, invest in a car charger so you always have your Kansas music on the road (see Figure 3.3).

Figure 3.3

Charge your iPod in the car.

Here's a quick list of some of the car chargers available with approximate pricing:

- DLO AutoPod AutoCharger (available for iPod, iPod mini, and iPod shuffle), $29.99
- Griffin PowerPod Auto Charger, $27.99
- XtremeMac Car Charger for iPod shuffle, $23.95

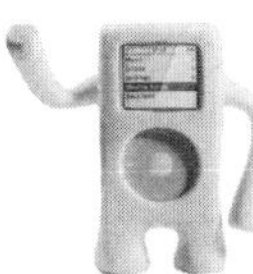

Tip

If you are going to listen to your iPod in the car, you might want it to have its own special seat or holder. You can find several iPod holders designed for the car. Belkin's TuneDok Car Holder has a suction cup that holds the iPod in position; the holder fits inside the car's cup holder. Akron also has a cup holder model as well as a mount kit for the car. These special holders cost $30–$35.

iPod Accessories for Sports

You've seen the many accessories you can outfit your iPod with for travel. But what about little trips like a skate around the block, a bike ride around the 'hood, or even a swim (yes, a swim!) in your local pool. Like a Barbie doll, the iPod includes special outfits for all of these adventures. You can find one to suit your hobby of choice.

For instance, running or working out is always more fun when you do it to music. To supply the tunes for your workouts, you need your iPod. To hold your iPod in place while you do your jumping jacks or downward facing dog (for yoga fans), you can look into an action jacket for your iPod. DLO's Action Jacket product is an adjustable armband with a special holder for your iPod; the price is $24.99. You can also attach your iPod to your belt via a clip with these jackets. You have still more choices…you can get different versions of the jacket for the iPod mini or iPod shuffle, and you can even select a special color or purchase elastic armbands in different colors to vary your look ($9.99).

XtremeMac offers a similar product named SportWrap, which provides skip-free music for bikers, joggers, and other workout routines. It costs around $30.

If you don't want to attach your iPod to your body, you can carry it in a convenient hand-held case, such as the HandSkin Active iPod case. And wait, there's more. What about swimmers (or wakeboarders, surfers, kayakers, and other water sports fans)? You can choose from the Audio Swimbelt for the iPod ($39.95), a belt that houses your iPod and that you wear around your waist; or the H2O Audio Armband, a waterproof armband-style holder for your iPod ($29.95). Like SpyKids, you are prepared for every situation with all of the various iPod holders on the market. But there's still more choices...

Carry It with You

To make it easy to tote your iPod with you, you have several options. For instance, you can add a clip and attach your iPod to your belt. Expect to pay $15 or so for a belt clip. The iPod shuffle comes with a lanyard that you wear around your neck. You can also purchase a lanyard and a swivel clip case to carry around your classic iPod. The lanyard is really cheap—$5—and it has cord snaps so you can connect your headphones and avoid tangles.

Another way to keep your iPod from wandering is to attach a hook to it; you can then attach the hook to your backpack strap, belt loop, purse strap, or to a keychain. Hooks designed to work with an iPod run around $20. Backpacks are also available now with special holders for iPods. You can take your tunes to school with your iPod conveniently stored in its own zippered pouch. Just make sure it stays there during class (or that Mrs. Pickard doesn't catch you listening to Coldplay during her *fascinating* lecture on *The Hobbit*).

Coming Attractions

This chapter covered some car-, travel-, and sports-related iPod accessories, but you still have other options for carrying and protecting your iPod. For instance, you can buy an iPod wallet or any number of cases to store or carry your iPod. Chapter 4, "Stylin' and Profilin': iPod Skins, Tattoos, Cases, and More," covers not only the style options these cases provide, but also how they can help protect your iPod from dings and scratches.

Chapter 4

Stylin' and Profilin': iPod Skins, Tattoos, Cases, and More

The tunes you play on your iPod aren't the same as your friends. They are your own personal collection of songs, artists, and music types, from rap to country, from old style to alternative. Why, then, should your iPod look like everyone else's? That's just it—it shouldn't.

Although Apple only offers a few colors and styles of iPods, you aren'tlimited to just these versions. Instead, you have lots of alternatives for changing how your iPod looks. You can choose from swappable tattoos or skins to wallets, travel cases, and purses. Are you the cute and cuddly type? How about an iPod sock? You can purchase one or knit your own. Are you the outdoor type?

Select from some of the seriously rugged versions for hiking, mountain climbing, kayaking, or just plain klutzing around.

With all the products available, you have a wide range of choices. And many of the options won't break your piggy bank. You can find cases for less than $20.

The various case and cover options provide protection as well as enable you to make your own personal style statement.

Add a Skin to Your iPod

Skins are like a little suit that your iPod sports to both look snazzy and to protect itself from scuffs, dirt, dust, and scratches. Usually the skin fits around the iPod pretty snuggly and includes cutouts so you can access the plugs, click wheel, and dock connector port. The display is covered with a clear screen protector so you can see it.

Note

You can also purchase removable skins. These are covered later in this section.

Heavy-Duty Skins

The types and styles of skin are many. Table 4.1 gives you some idea of the popular products available. Keep in mind that the list isn't comprehensive and that prices might vary. Still, you can get an idea of what's on the market by skimming through this list.

Table 4.1 iPod Skins

Product	Purchase At	Price
iSkin eVo2 Wild Sides (see Figure 4.1)	www.iskin.com, www.theistore.com, or http://thinkdifferent store.com	$29.99–$34.99
iSkin eVo	www.iskin.com or www.theistore.com	$29.99
Xskin eXoflip	www.theistore.com	$24
Xskin eXo2	www.theistore.com	$34.99

Figure 4.1

iSkin eVo2 Wild Sides is a popular skin, and it comes with a belt clip that rotates.

Caution

If you don't want to purchase an entire skin cover, you can get a screen protector for your display. These cost around $10 and usually are simply clear adhesive covers. Some come with a screen cleaning cloth. (For more on cleaning and maintaining your iPod, see Chapter 12, "Maintain It: Chargers, Batteries, and Clean Up.")

Sticker Skins and Wraps

If you want a less expensive option or a skin that you can swap as your mood changes, you can purchase skins or wraps that are like stickers. These often come in sets of several designs. Some are fully adhesive; others have adhesive corners that attach to your iPod. All claim that they leave no sticky residue (but you'll probably have to test that for yourself).

At designerskins.com, you can find a wide variety of skins for various electronic devices including GameCube, PS/2, XBox, and iPods. You have a wide variety of choices including abstract, animal, fantasy, holographic, scenic, and sci-fi (to name a few). Expect to pay around $6.99 for this type of skin (see Figure 4.2).

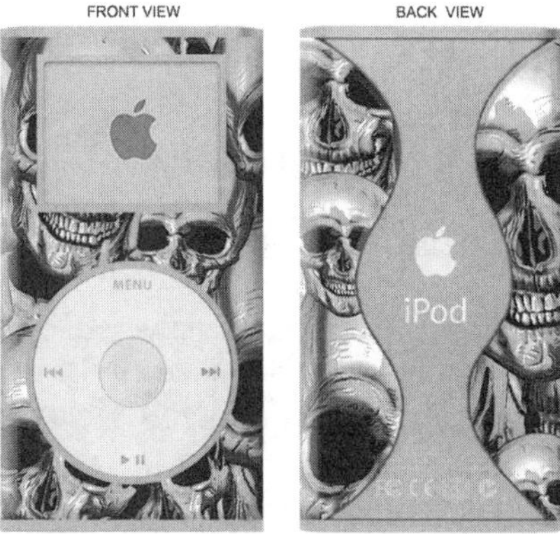

Figure 4.2

Skulls Inside is just one of the "crazy" skins available at designerskins.com.

Another source for skins are wraps, available at thinkdifferentstore.com. These durable, water-resistant wraps last about a month and include instructions for applying the wrap. Again, you can pick a style that matches your mood or personality. How about a tie-dye version? The cost is reasonable ($5), so maybe you can buy several!

These aren't your only choices. You can also investigate Podskinz. Or if you want a clear, super-thin wrap that shows your iPod in all it's natural glory, try the PodShield (both available at thinkdifferentstore.com). This product comes in pieces that you attach, and it costs roughly $13.

iPoDonuts

What if you just want your click wheel to stand out? In that case, you can buy an iPoDonut. It not only protects your click wheel from scratches, but it also glows in the dark. Now you can listen to your iPod under your covers when you should be asleep. You can select from a variety of styles (see Figure 4.3). Just visit the iPoDonut site (www.ipodonut.com) and find your favorite donut.

Figure 4.3

Light up your click wheel with an iPoDonut from the site with the same name.

Tattoo Your iPod

Another option is an iPod tattoo. Although your parents might not let you get a body tattoo, they'll likely agree to an iPod tattoo. These iPod covers are inexpensive and durable, *and* they protect your case and screen from scratches and scuffs. Another cool thing—you can change them so you aren't stuck with one design or one look. After all, you don't wear the same outfit everyday. (Well, maybe you do, but that's none of my business.)

A tattoo is basically a template that you print on special paper created and sold by Hewlett-Packard; after you print the template, you can cut out the template (as well as the area for the click wheel) and then wrap it around, adhering it to your iPod. Get tired of one look? Take off the current tattoo and replace it with a new one. Hewlett-Packard says that the tattoo should stay affixed for about a month if you leave it on without changing it.

The paper is the vehicle for tricking out your iPod, but the design is the key to your own self-expression. You can download predesigned tattoos and use them for your iPod. You can view several iPod tattoos online. For instance, HP includes a gallery of several styles.

Also, at My iPod Tattoos (http://my-ipod-tattoos.com), you can view current designs and collections, including (at the time this book was written) Christmas tattoos. You can find designs with stars, military camouflage, snowmen, stripes, bubbles, and more. Scroll through all the pages, checking out designs. See one you like? Use the links to purchase and download designs. Or order a complete collection on CD so you can share designs with friends. Costs for tattoos range from $7.77 to $19.99, depending on the design or collection. You can also find and purchase these same tattoos at RadioShack or Circuit City and at other online sites.

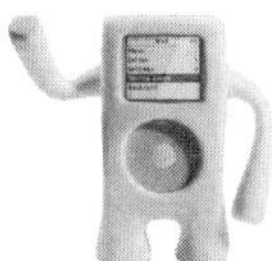

Tip

HP says that the template works with most inkjet printers. If you want to see whether yours will work, check the tattoo printing instructions. You can find instructions online as well as on the package. Also note that the template only works with regular printer sizes (*not* 4" × 6" printers).

You can buy the paper at office supply and computer stores or online at Hewlett-Packard (www.shopping.hp.com). The price at the online store is $13.49 (plus shipping and handling). The paper includes the appropriate instructions for printing the tattoo. You'll need an inkjet printer cable of printing the template. So load the paper, open the design, and follow along.

Tip

If you want to be *very* unique, you can design your own iPod tattoo, drawing on the paper or creating a digital design. This process is pretty complex and requires an image-editing program such as

Adobe Photoshop Elements. With this program, you can draw objects, insert special characters, add color, scan photos, and more. If you are up for the challenge and know some basics about working in photo programs, check out the instructions included with the tattoo paper.

Cases, Purses, Wallets, Oh My!

Chapter 3, "Take It with You: iPod Travel Accessories," covered some carrying options for your iPod, but this chapter provides all of the options for keeping your iPod with you, keeping it safe, and keeping it stylin'. Girls can pick from pink metallic wallets; guys might opt for rugged jam jackets. If you are searching for something to carry your iPod, you're likely to find a suitable option in this section. So "carry" on.

Cases for Your iPod

If you are the simple sort, you might opt for a simple case. But the decision on *which* simple case might not be so simple. All cases promise protection from scratches, dust, dirt, and other pollutants. All offer some way to attach the case to your body (usually through a belt clip). Most come in a variety of colors. The differences boil down to what the case is made of and the price. Although Table 4.2 doesn't mention every case on the market, it does give you some products to start with and to compare with others you find during your own hunting.

Table 4.2 iPod Cases

Product	Purchase At	Price
Speck ToughSkin (see Figure 4.4)	http://everythingipod.com, http://thinkdifferentstore.com	$24.50–$34.95
DLO Jam Jacket	http://everythingipod.com	$24.99 ($12.99 sale price)
Contour iSee	http://everythingipod.com	$19.95
PodSleevz	http://thinkdifferentstore.com	$19.95
iShield	http://thinkdifferentstore.com	$34.99 ($19.99 sale price)
Lilipod Hardshell Case	http://thinkdifferentstore.com	$39.95
OtterBox Waterproof Case	http://thinkdifferentstore.com	Check online for pricing

Product	Purchase At	Price
Incase Neoprene Sleeve	http://store.apple.com	$19.95
Agent 18 MiniShield	http://store.apple.com	$19.95
Marware SportSuit Safari for iPod mini	http://everything ipod.com	$19.95

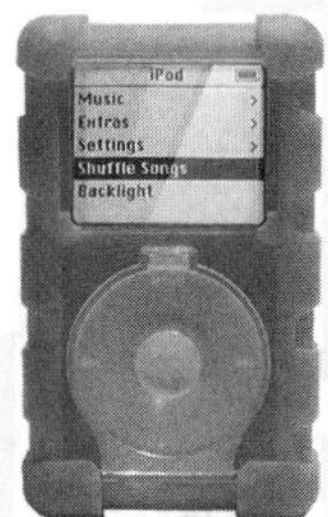

Figure 4.4

The Speck ToughSkin is a good rugged case available in several colors.

Wallets and Purses

For those who want to carry a little something extra with their iPod, a wallet, purse, or case with space might be just the ticket. Guys, don't despair. While there are some girlie purse and wallet options, there are also some choices for the dudes as well. Again, use Table 4.3 to see what's available. Then make out your shopping wish list.

Table 4.3 iPod Wallets and Purses

Product	Purchase At	Price
Marware Sportsuit Convertible	http://store.apple.com	$39.95
Cocoon iPod Case (see Figure 4.5)	http://thinkdifferent store.com	$39.95
Case Closed Sheldon Leather iPod Case	www.ebags.com	$29.99
Magnesium iPod Case	http://thinkdifferent store.com	$34.99
iPod Wallet (see Figure 4.6)	http://thinkdifferent store.com or http://everything ipod.com	$59.99 (iPod), $44.99 (iPod mini)
DLO Executive Podfolio	http://everything ipod.com	$39.99
DLO mini Fling for iPod mini (see Figure 4.7)	http://everything ipod.com or www.dlo.com	$34.99

Product	Purchase At	Price
DLO Podsling Leather iPod mini Carry-all Case	http://everything ipod.com or www.dlo.com	$34.99

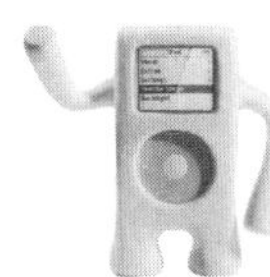

Tip

For the ultra-trendy, get a Louis Vuitton Monogrammed cover ($215 at www.eluxury.com) or one made from Coach suede ($68, available where Coach items are sold).

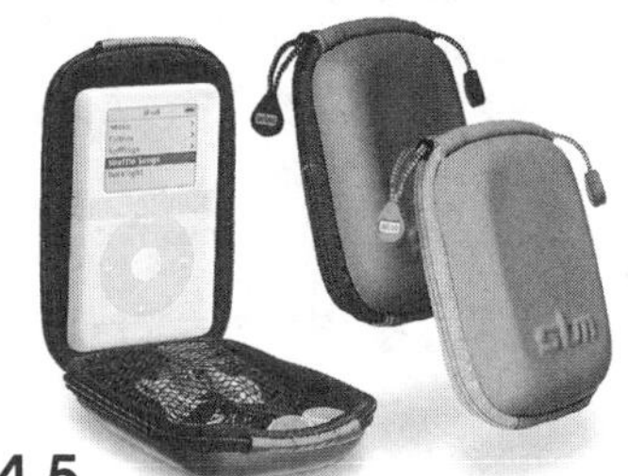

Figure 4.5

If you want a sturdy case with room to store your earbuds, try the Cocoon iPod Case.

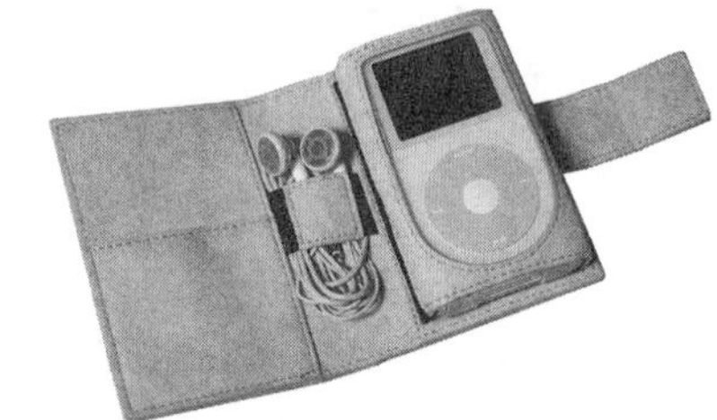

Figure 4.6

Carry your iPod wallet separately or put it inside your purse or backpack.

Figure 4.7

Stash your cash, lip gloss, and iPod mini in this wallet.

Special iPod Shuffle Covers

The iPod shuffle, with its skinny frame and no display, has different options available to protect and carry it. Some protection products to consider if this is the type of iPod you own include

- **Xtreme Mac TuffWrapz**—Durable cover for both shuffle caps. Available in sets of three (lemon, bubble gum, and grape; sky, tangerine, or lime; or cobalt, mist, or cherry). $24.95 at www.theistore.com.
- **Xtreme Max Shieldz**—Secures iPod to lanyard and protects it from nicks, dings, and scratches. Available also in sets of three (similar colors as the TuffWrapz). $19.95 at www.theistore.com.
- **DLO Jam Jacket**—Silicone cases for the iPod shuffle for protection and to make it easier to grip. Comes in three flavors: Purple, Glow Green, and Frosty Clear. $29.99 at www.everythingipod.com.
- **DLO Jam Caps**—A set of five caps that slip on your USB port and add color and style. $19.99 at www.everythingipod.com.

Travel Cases

Toting around your iPod and headphones is one thing. Taking along all of your iPod supplies is another. For those times when you'll be away from home (camp? Grandma's house?), you might want a more full-featured case. One, for instance, that includes a charger. In this case, you might opt for the large RoadWired Pod Pouch ($19.96 at www.ebags.com). It includes six or more pockets and compartments, including a "secret" pocket for cash or keys. You can pick your favorite color.

If you want something more compact, consider Monster's iCase Travel Pack; this includes a place to store your iPod and earphones, but also the Monster iCarCharger and the Monster iSplitter (see Chapter 2, "Listen Up: iPod Audio Gear," for details on this product). It also includes pockets and compartments for other necessities (see Figure 4.8). You can purchase this for roughly $70 at www.thinkdifferentstore.com.

Another option is the Incase Travel Kit for all iPods ($59.95 at http://store.apple.com). This includes pockets for your iPod accessories and a charger as well as pockets for a plane ticket and passport. Are you heading abroad? Then this is the case for you!

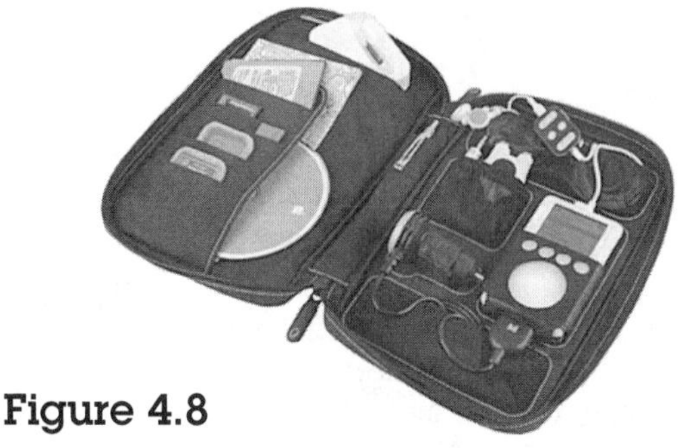

Figure 4.8

For those trips away from home, consider a full travel pack with charger and other storage pockets.

Fun, Funky, and Fashion-Forward

If you've read this far, you might think that there can't possibly be yet more options, but there are! In fact, this is the fun, funky, fashion-conscious, forward section. So if you dare to be different, consider one of these special covers:

- How about a Delapod bag, a specially designed purse that lets you access your iPod from one side of the purse. Turn it the other way and it's a plain, trendy-looking purse. Visit www.delapod.com to view designs.
- Are you a sock freak? Then you can outfit your iPod in a sock, also. While these don't provide as much protection as some of the other case options, they are cute and cuddly. Buy them at http://store.apple.com in a set with a variety of colors ($29.99).

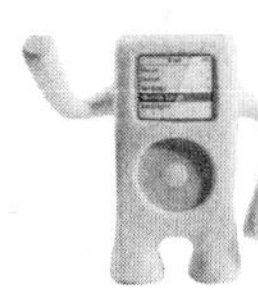

Tip

If you are the crafty type, you can knit your own iPod sock. You can find patterns at www.lionbrand.com.

- How about a crocheted case? You can order one in a variety of colors at www.beckysbeads.com for $12 (see Figure 4.9).

Figure 4.9

Pick out the yarn for your own crocheted cover at Becky's Beads.

- Or what about a hoodie? Or a Santa Sock (thinkdifferent.com)? Expect other types of covers to pop up as iPods become an everyday device.

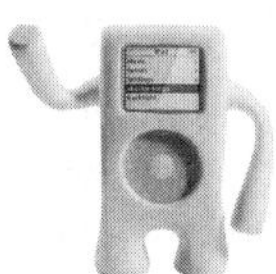

Tip

Try searching online for iPod covers, iPod socks, or whatever type of cover you seek. You can then check out the online sites that offer these and other new products.

- If you like the Cousin It look, you might order a Wild Pocket. (No, they don't go in the microwave.) Like other funk-a-delic options, you can order this cover in a variety of colors (see Figure 4.10). Plus the pocket is washable.

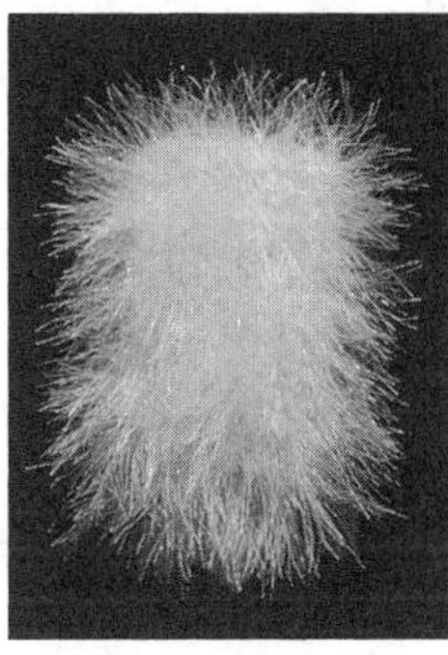

Figure 4.10

This wild cover is sure to get attention!

Custom Bling for the Rich and Famous

And finally, last but not least, are the Paris Hilton-type covers. You can find several sites that will bling bling your iPod with Swarovski crystals. You can purchase kits where you apply the crystals (you chose the colors). Or you can send in your iPod and let the company do the glitter-fy-ing. You can search for offers at eBay, check out www.ioffer.com, or visit www.crystalicing.com (see Figure 4.11). All those sparkles don't come cheap. Expect to pay $180 or more.

If you want just a tad of bling, you can purchase jewelry (yes, jewelry!) for your iPod. The designs and materials vary; you can contact the artist and get pricing and design information at www.ipodjewelry.com.

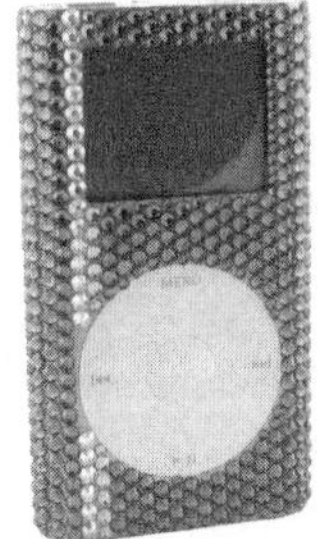

Figure 4.11

Add crystals to your iPod to really make a fashion statement! (Photo provided by and copyrighted by crystalicing.com.)

And for those who just have to have a one-of-a-kind iPod, you can create an Etch-a-Sketch style design (or choose from ones such as popular sports teams or bands) and ETCHamac.com will etch the design onto your iPod. Check their site (www.etchamac.com) for pricing and ordering details (see Figure 4.12).

Figure 4.12

Pick out an etch-a-sketch design for your iPod or create your own at ETCHamac.com.

Coming Attractions

We've covered taking your iPod on the road or just carrying it to school, to sports practice, to friend's houses, to parties, or to wherever. Now you are due for a rest. What about just simply staying at home? Where can you provide a place of honor for your iPod when you and it are lounging at su casa (that's your home, for the non-Spanish speakers)?

Chapter 5

Hangin' at Your Crib: iPod Docks and Remotes

Sure, you are on the go most of the time. That's part of what makes the iPod so cool: You always have your entire music collection right in your pocket. Even so, you do spend *some* time at home. When you go to sleep, are grounded, need to charge your iPod, update your music through iTunes, do homework, hang with friends, and so on. For keeping your iPod charged and connected at home, you can look into some home accessories, including stands to hold your iPod, docks to charge your iPod and connect it to your computer or to other devices, and a remote so you can change the tune without movin' your bod. Think of this as the Home Depot chapter for the iPod. What home improvements do you need for your iPod home?

Standing Around

When you listen to your iPod while working on your homework or just lounging around, you might not want to hold it. Instead prop it in a handy stand. From the funky new iGuy to a sleek podboard, a stand makes it easy to view the iPod screen and access the controls.

iGuy

One of the newer products to pop up on the market is the iGuy, a protective case with bendable arms (see Figure 5.1). Like the cases covered in Chapter 4, "Stylin' and Profilin': iPod Skins, Tattoos, Cases, and More," it includes a screen protector and access to all of your controls. But this iGuy can stand, sit (his butt has dock access so that you can charge or sync tunes when he sits down on a dock), and hold things in his Gumby-like arms. Much more fun than a plain old case! You can find iGuy hanging at http://thinkdifferentstore.com.

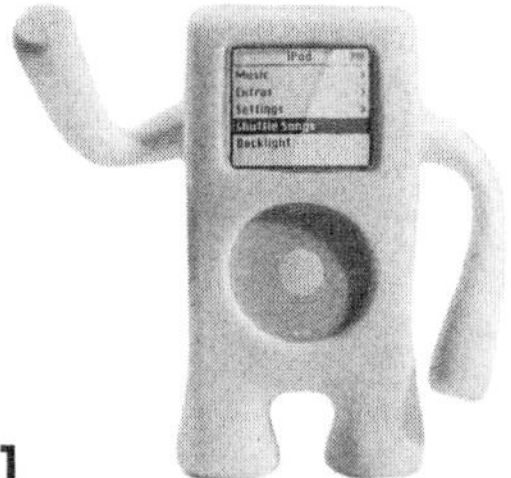

Figure 5.1

The iGuy can stand, sit, and hold things in his bendable arms.

Podboard

If the iGuy is a little too cutesy for you, you might be more interested in a different type of stand. How about the sleek podboard made of stainless steel (see Figure 5.2)? The clips on the back hold the iPod in place and also provide a convenient spot to hold your cables. You can adjust the angle of the board so you can view it while working on your computer or just sitting at your desk thinking about writing that paper. Like other cases, the podboard provides protection from scratches and access to controls. You can even carry your podboard with you or customize it with different designs. Like what you see? If so, you can order a podboard at www.alscher.ch.

Figure 5.2

You can adjust the podboard to any angle for easy viewing.

Note:

The podboard does not work with iPod mini or iPod shuffle.

PodStyle and PodHolder

Similar products to the podboard include the PodStyle and PodHolder. The PodStyle stand is made from aluminum and includes a pocket lined with padding for protection. The PodHolder is a clear acrylic stand. You can find both at http://thinkdifferentstore.com.

For a complete housing unit (with stand), consider the Bubble Design Habitat Stand. Angled for easy viewing (like the other stands), the Habitat also provides access to the controls. In their words the habitat provides "one-handed operation of the iPod in its elegant new home." (Here's a new show idea for MTV: Cribs for iPods.) It also includes rubber feet so it doesn't slide around. (It might decide to take a stroll across your desk. You wouldn't want it to slip and fall!) You can find more about this stand at http://everythingipod.com.

iPod Docks

A dock is like a stand, but it has a more useful purpose than simply holding your iPod upright. When you place your iPod into the dock, you can sync your tunes and also charge your iPod. The iPod sits in the dock, and you run cables from the back of the dock to your computer (see Figure 5.3). It's a useful home base for your iPod.

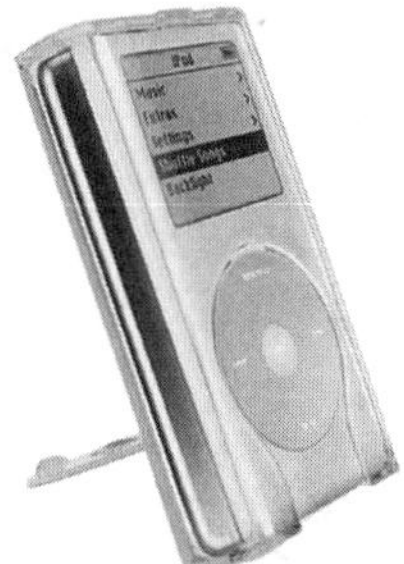

Figure 5.3

Use your dock as your home base and sync and charge your iPod from the dock.

How do the docks differ? One difference is that some docks fit only one iPod model. In this case, you need to be sure you get a dock that's designed for your particular iPod (iPod, iPod mini, iPod nano, or iPod shuffle). Most docks provide ports for connecting via a USB cable and port or a FireWire cable and port. Check to be sure the dock you want has the ports and cables that work with your computer. Some also provide other ports such as an AV port for connecting your iPod to a TV.

Tip:
Most new computers include both USB and FireWire ports, but some older computers might not have FireWire ports. Check with your computer documentation to see the types of ports you have.

Portable Docks

In addition to stay-at-home docks, you can also find portable docks that plug into the iPod's docking port and then provide access ports for other cables. For instance, the PocketDock lets you connect to other devices and accessories through a FireWire cable. It's kind of a cable middleman; plug it into your iPod's docking port and then plug other cables into the PocketDock. Find this product at www.theistore.com ($18.95).

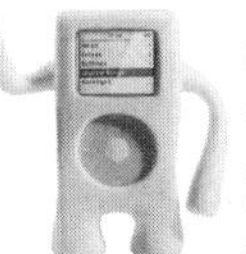

Tip:

You can also purchase docks that have ports for S-video and RCA cables. You can use these types of ports and cables to connect your iPod to a TV. For instance, PodsPlus (www.podsplus.com) offers a dock with a video-out port ($39.99). Connected to a TV or a computer with an S-video port, you can view pictures or slide-shows while listening to music. Chapter 6, "Music and More," provides more details on musicalslideshows.

Caution:

Other accessories for your iPod include batteries, chargers, and cables. You can read up on these in Chapter 12, "Maintain It: Chargers, Batteries, and Clean Up."

Remote Control

If you are listening to your iPod while it's docked, in a stand, or even across the room on your dresser, you don't have to get up to change the volume or skip to a different song. Naw, that would be wasting too much energy! Instead, you can add a remote to your iPod. The remote receiver plugs into the top of the iPod. Then you use the little hand-held remote to control the volume, skip to another song, replay a song, stop the music, or turn off the iPod.

Caution:

You can select an artist or playlist from the iPod and then scroll from song to song from the list, but you can't change to a specific song or playlist using the remote. You can control only the songs lined up to be played.

Here's a quick look at some of the various remote options on the market:

- **DLO iDirect Remote Control**—Includes the remote receiver and a five-button remote (see Figure 5.4). $39.99.

Figure 5.4

Add remote control to your iPod.

- **TEN Technology NaviPod Wireless Remote Control**—Also includes a five-button remote with Play/Pause, Next, Previous, and Volume buttons. It also comes with a chrome stand. $49.95.
- **Airclick iPod Remote**—Uses signals that travel through walls so you can control your iPod from inside or outside the house, up to 60 feet away. Also has an iPod mini version. $34.99.

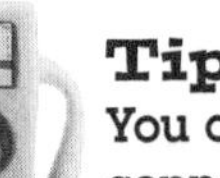

Tip:
You can also get remotes for iPods connected to speakers or a stereo (even your car stereo). These options are covered in Chapter 3, "Take It with You: iPod Travel Accessories."

Although this last product isn't a remote, it does provide the same type of access to your iPod music. The Control Relocator attaches to the top of the iPod so you can play, pause, skip, repeat, or change the volume from the top of the iPod. This is handy if you want to keep your iPod in your pocket (kind of sneaky!) or in a case or purse. You can find this product at everythingi-pod.com, and it costs roughly $30.

Coming Attractions

So far in this book you've seen all the add-ons for better listening, for playing the iPod through a stereo or car, for toting your iPod around in style, and for housing the iPod in its own holder at home. Now let's get into the actual music!

Chapter 6

Music and More

Of course the main purpose of your iPod is music, and the place to most easily purchase that music is through iTunes. But what else can you do to add to and improve the music experience?

One thing is to create playlists; this lets you create sets of songs. Maybe you have songs you like to listen to when you are sad. Or perhaps there are songs that get you pumped for a game. You might have a party mix or a romance mix. In any case, you can learn how to best set up your playlists using iPod features, as well as some mini-programs designed to work on the iPod.

And what if you are a budding singer? Wouldn't having the lyrics available make singing along easier? Lyrics can also prove disputes with friends over the *real* words. You can view and display the actual song lyrics in iTunes and on your iPod.

Want more? What about visual stimulation? You can find a variety of visual imagery to display while you are listening to your music, starting with album art. You can also create CD cover cases that include song lists, album art, or other information.

One of the newest cool things to do is to listen to *podcasts*—radio programs distributed via iTunes. Unlike live radio broadcasts, you can listen to a podcast at any time. This chapter also introduces you to this growing phenomenon.

Finally, we'll explore still other options for your iPod, including language translations. The world of iPod and iTunes expands every day! So get started on what's hip today.

iTunes

Apple's iTunes Music Store includes more than 1.5 million songs! And some songs are available exclusively at iTunes (which means you can't download these songs at any other site). Let's take a look at some things you can do at the site that helps you get and organize the music you want:

- Do you want to know when the new Kayne West CD comes out? Sign up for Artist Alerts, and iTunes will email you when the CD (or songs from the CD) are available.

- What do the stars listen to? Check out Celebrity playlists. These include not only their recommendations, but also notes about their picks.
- View the top songs and albums based on what other people are buying and listening to in the Top Selling lists on the iTunes site.
- Listen to samples of songs. Just because your favorite artist has a new song doesn't mean you'll like it. Listen first. Buy when you know you like the song.
- Watch full-length videos or movie trailers.
- Email your friends a link about a new album.
- For your friend's birthday, what about a gift certificate to iTunes? Or tell your Aunt Maureen (who got you cocoa for your last birthday) that you sure would *love* an iTunes gift certificate.

This list might be a reminder of what you already know (but sometimes you just know the basics or forget about everything that's available). Now let's look in detail at some things you might not know about.

Making Cool Playlists

You probably already know about playlists, but did you know some of the ways you can more easily create them? Did you know that you can post your own special playlist at the iTunes store so others can view your top music selections? If not, read this section to get the inside edition on playlists.

Sharing Your Playlists

You might consider yourself a music expert. Maybe your friends constantly ask you about what you listen to. If you are the expert DJ mix master, consider sharing your knowledge with your friends and other iTunes visitors.

You can create a special playlist (or use one of your existing ones). Then publish the iMix to the iTunes store where it will be available for one year. You can even add your own notes about why a particular song is special or why you placed two songs together. Then you can email your list to friends, rate and view other iMixes, and listen to what others say about your iMix.

Create Playlists Based on Ratings, Lyrics, and More

Although you can manually add songs to a playlist as you expand your music collection, you might wish there was an easier way. You have lots of options. If you rate your tunes, you can create a playlist based on tunes with a certain rating. You can also search for songs based on lyrics. For instance, you can search for and create a playlist based on all songs that mention Memphis in the lyrics or all songs that include the word *love*.

Your iPod automatically tracks stuff such as when you last played a song, any comments you've added, how many times you've played a song, and your rating. When you sync your iPod with iTunes, you can create smart playlists from these stats. To make this feature worthwhile, you have to regularly remember to rate songs you listen to. Here's how to do it:

1. While listening to the song, press the Select button twice. You see stars onscreen.
2. Use the click wheel to increase or decrease the star rating.

From iTunes, you can select ratings as well as other criteria on which to base a playlist. Follow these steps:

1. From iTunes, click the File menu and then select New Smart Playlist.
2. In the Smart Playlist dialog box, click the first drop-down list (see Figure 6.1).

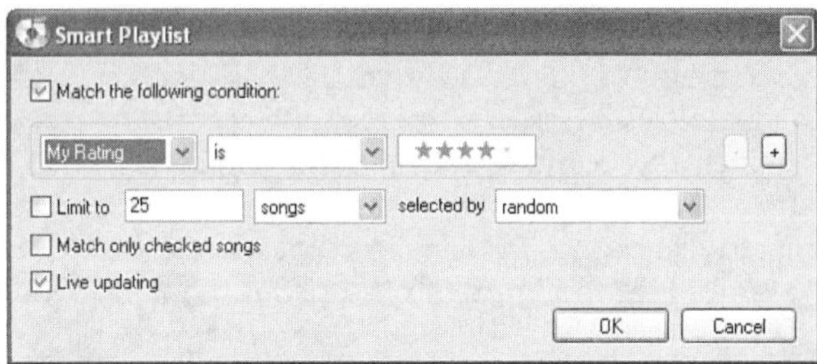

Figure 6.1

Rate your songs and then create a playlist of just your top songs.

3. Click My Rating.
4. Click the second drop-down list and select = (equal to). iTunes automatically selects five stars as the rating to match.
5. If you want to match a lesser number, click a star, starting from the right, until you end up with the number of stars you want (shown previously in Figure 6.1).
6. Click OK to create your playlist.

Tip

If you don't want to rank all your tunes, you can use iRate, a freeware program, available at www.apple.com/downloads/macosx/ipod_itunes/irate.html, that calculates a ranking based on play count, ranking, and how long the track has been in your library.

In addition to the features of iTunes, you can also use other utility programs to expand the capabilities. With PlayLyrix, you can automatically create a playlist of songs with lyrics that include a word or phrase. Create a birthday-themed list, for instance, by selecting all tunes that include *birthday*. You can get this shareware program at www.apple.com/downloads/macosx/ipod_itunes/playlyrix.html.

Your tunes are tagged as a type of music: country, rock, and so on. But sometimes these aren't descriptive enough. For instance, there's new country (Kenny Chesney, Brad Paisley) and then old country (Tammy Wynette, Merle Haggard). You might want to distinguish between the two (as well as other music types). If so, check out TuneTags. You can use the tags supplied with the library or create your own tags (see Figure 6.2). Visit www.apple.com/downloads/macosx/ipod_itunes/tunetags.html to download this shareware program.

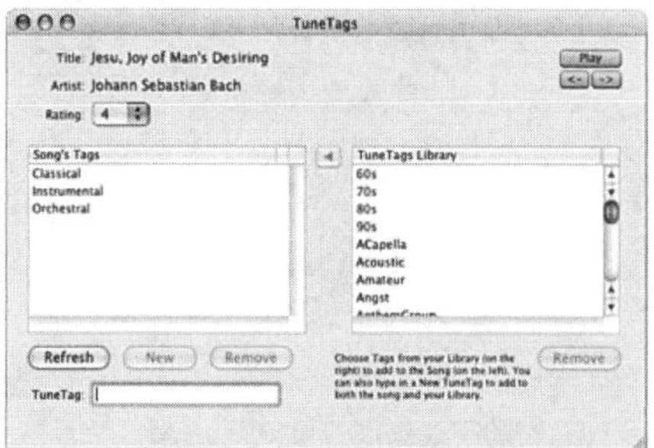

Figure 6.2

Tag your tunes with more descriptive tags by using Tune Tags.

Creating CDs and Cases

When you purchase music, iTunes also downloads the album art. If you create a CD from an album, you can create a cover with the art and the track listing. More commonly, though, you might create custom CDs with tunes from various albums and artists. In this case, iTunes will automatically create a case with a mosaic of relevant album art and a listing of songs. If that look isn't fly enough for you, use one of iTunes templates and build your own professional-looking covers (see Figure 6.3). For instance, you can use your own artwork on the cover.

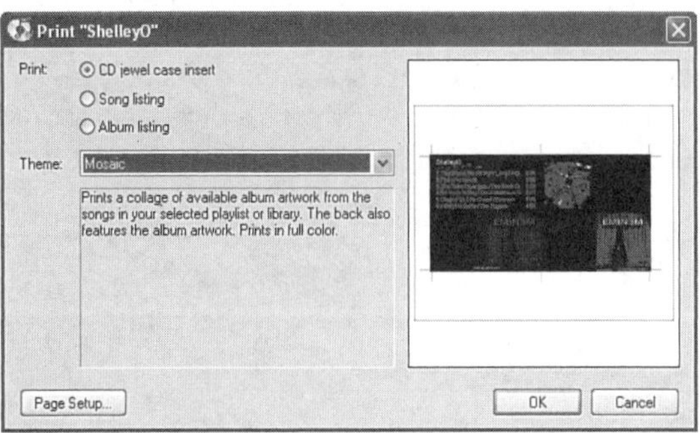

Figure 6.3

Print your own CD cases selecting one of the predefined templates.

Singing Along to the Song

Many CD liners include the song lyrics so you can read the exact lyrics (instead of figuring them out yourself, especially for those mumbley-type or screaming singers). For instance, it took me forever to figure out what they were saying in the B52's "Love Shack:" It's *tin roof rusted*. Go figure!

Keeping all your CD cases and liners defeats the purpose of conveniently storing your music, so if you want lyrics, you can use one of several lyric programs found at www.apple.com/downloads/macosx/ipod_itunes/:

- When you play a song in iTunes, you can use Search Lyrictracker, which does just that: It searches the Lyrictracker database and displays the results on a web page. New in the current version, you can limit the search to an artist or song title (regardless of the artist).
- With KaraTunes, you can not only view the lyrics, but you can edit them. You can also upload the lyrics to your iPod; this program also searches the Lyrictracker database (see Figure 6.4).
- With pearLyrics, you can look up the lyrics without playing the songs. To do so, you need to enter the artist and song title. Also, this program consults several databases to find the lyrics.

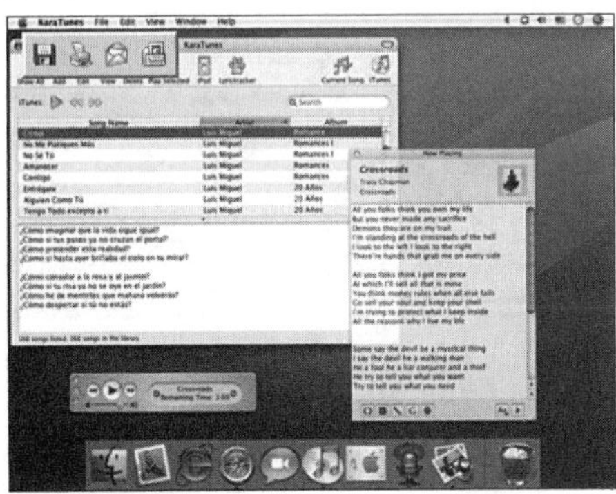

Figure 6.4

Find and view lyrics of your fave tunes.

Tip

If you are a guitar player, pearLyrics can even get the guitar cords for some tunes. And to play along with songs, consider the JamPod. This includes a small guitar amplifier that you can plug into your iPod and practice along with songs. The JamPod costs roughly $50 and is available at http://thinkdifferentstore.com.

- In addition to lyrics, Utilitunes will fetch some album artwork.
- iLyric enables you to search the Internet for the lyrics to music in your collection. You can also download the lyrics to your iPod.

And what if you want a companion to listen (and dance!) along with you as you jam to your iPod? The iDog is not only a fun music toy, but it's also a composer and works as a speaker (see Figure 6.5). Here's how it works: Plug it into your headphones, and the iDog will rock and roll by moving its head and ears as well as let you know what it thinks of your music. (Based on the music, the seven LED lights flash in rhythm using different color combinations.) You can also place the iDog in front of speakers to watch it dance. The iDog remembers 70 songs and can create its own music based on the music you've "fed" it.

The iDog costs a little less than $30, uses three AAA batteries, and works with the iPod as well as other portable music players. You can find the iDog at Amazon.com as well as online toy and electronic sites. The next section covers some other alternatives to visualizing your music.

Figure 6.5

The iDog can be your dance partner and music critic, and you don't even have to clean up after it.

Visualizing the Music (with Some Help)

Sure, you can close your eyes and conjure up images from the music being played, but maybe you need a little help. Plus, it's cool to see how different programs can combine images into effects such as a kaleidoscope. You can also find art from an album and display it on your iPod or use it on your computer (to create CD inserts, for instance, mentioned in earlier in this chapter).

Two available visualization programs include Kaleidostrobe (displays kaleidoscopic patterns) and Eyephedrine (see Figure 6.6). You can find both at www.apple.com/downloads/macosx/ipod_itunes/kaleidostrobe.html and www.apple.com/downloads/macosx/ipod_itunes/eyephedrine.html.

Figure 6.6

Motion blur, light bloom, and other technical features combine to create the visualizations for Eyephedrine.

Tip
Usually these programs work best with music with a heavy beat.

To manage artwork for individual songs and albums, you can use the iTunesCool program. With this utility, you can search and fetch artwork, export artwork to common file formats (so you can use them in other documents), and remove artwork from selected tracks. This shareware program is available at www.apple.com/downloads/macosx/ipod_itunes/itunescool.html.

Managing Your Music Collection

A few utility programs can help you manage your music. For instance, with PodLock, you can do the following:

- Speed up your iPod so songs load faster by optimizing your iPod with a tool called a defragmenter.
- Hide important files (useful if you use your iPod to store data or picture files, the topic of Chapter 11, "Storing Data and Pictures on Your iPod").
- Back up and restore your iPod files.

You can get a demo of this program by going to www.apple.com/downloads and then searching for Podlock using that page's search tool.

If you want to create a web version of your library, consider iTunes catalog. The web version automatically includes links to music websites such as MTV and Rolling Stone. You can also add your own custom links (see Figure 6.7).

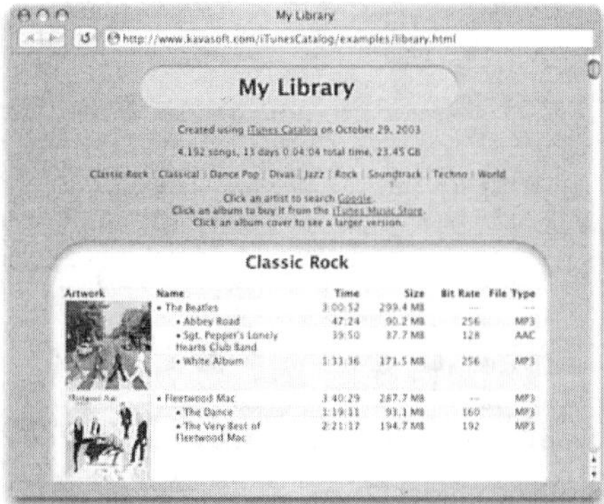

Figure 6.7

Create a web catalog of your music collection complete with links to popular music sites.

If you use the SonicSwap site, you might also add SonicSwap's myTunes, a replacement/add-on to iTunes. Membership to the SonicSwap.com website and the program for managing songs at this site are free. You can get more information by going to www.apple.com/downloads and then searching for this program.

Checking Out Podcasts

Apple defines podcasting as "radio your way." Why? Because you can listen to what you want when you want wherever you want on your iPod. Podcasting is a new type of Internet radio broadcasting, and podcasts are created by news and sports sources (ABC and ESPN) and radio shows (Daily Source Code with Adam Curry). But really these traditional players came late to the scene. Podcasting was started by ordinary people (or extraordinary people, really) who had a voice and wanted others to hear their opinions, entertainment, news, or whatever they wanted to include in their podcast or radio show. Users created their radio show and then uploaded the content to the Internet. Then their audience downloaded the show from the Internet to an iPod (or other player).

iTunes includes the following features for introducing you to the world of podcasting:

- Browse through the iTunes Podcast Directory and see what programs are available (more than 8,000 free podcasts). Figure 6.8 shows iTunes Podcast Directory.
- Sample the podcasts to see whether they are worth your listening time, and if so, subscribe to them. iTunes checks and downloads new episodes when you are a subscriber.

Figure 6.8

Find and listen to your favorite podcasts.

- Listen to podcasts from iTunes or on your iPod.

Tip

If you are really ambitious, you might consider creating your own podcast. iTunes includes a tutorial. And if you do create one, you can publish it at the iTunes site. You can find information and links to these features at www.apple.com/podcasting/.

Coming Attractions

If you are tired of using your iPod just to listen, consider what you can do when you add a recorder to your iPod. Record your own tunes. Record reminders to yourself. Use your recorder and iPod to create a podcast. You learn about these possibilities in the next chapter.

Chapter 7

Recording with Your iPod

What if you don't always want to listen to someone else? What if you have your own thoughts and ideas you want to express? What if you'd like to hear your own version of your favorite tune? In this case, you can record yourself and listen to your own singing, rhyming, talking, or whatever.

You might also find a recorder useful for school and school projects. For instance, you can record a class lecture. Or you might practice speaking a foreign language using a recorder. Or create an oral presentation, such as a book report. (Your parents will love the many academic features of a recorder!)

What's Fun or Useful About Recording?

Your iPod recorder works similar to a tape recorder. You

use a microphone to record the sound (your voice, your dog barking, and so on), and then you can play it back.

Here are some ideas to get you thinking about the fun and practical uses of using your iPod as a recorder. You might record

- **Reminder lists**—Do you keep lists of things you have to do, such as homework projects or household chores? Rather than write a to-do list, record one!
- **Teachers**—Especially in junior high and beyond, recording the teacher as he talks can help you when you review for tests or if you want to use class information for a report or other project.

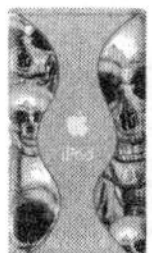

Caution

You'll need to check with your teacher to see whether it's okay to record your classes. Also, don't rely only on the recording. You still need to actively listen and take notes. Your iPod isn't an excuse for not paying attention in class!

- **Class discussions**—When everyone is talking at once, you might miss ideas. Also, discussions can jump from topic to topic. With a recording, you can organize the ideas that came up.

- **Practice foreign language sessions**—You can record assignments in Spanish, French, or whatever language you study. Play them back and evaluate yourself. This is a great way to improve your foreign language abilities and maybe even improve your grade.
- **Interviews**—You might do an interview for a class project, such as talking with someone that participated in the Vietnam War for a history project. You can also have some fun. Be your own David Letterman and interview your friends for your own talk show. You might turn out to be the next teen MTV star with your own show!
- **Oral presentations and projects**—Record yourself when practicing for oral presentations, such as a poetry reading, an oral book report, or a speech.
- **Conversations**—Remember a special night or event by recording your thoughts as well as the thoughts of your friends. For example, you might record silly stuff at a slumber party.
- **Your latest, greatest brainstorm**—When you have a great idea, don't wait until you can write it down. Record it instead.

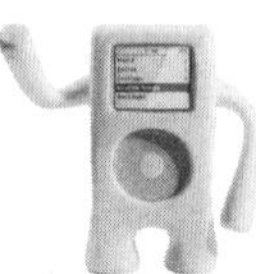

Tip

Are you a budding lawyer? Consider recording arguments or disagreements so you have an accurate record of what he said/she said. You then have proof that you definitely told your little brother he could not borrow your iPod.

- **Performances**—Record your singing, rapping, poetry, comedy routine, piano recital, or other performance. It's never too early to become a star, even if it's in your own mind!
- **The sounds of nature**—You might be interested in recording birds chirping for your own listening pleasure or for a science project. Croaking frogs might make you laugh, so record these silly sounds. You might record falling rain, ocean waves, or other soothing sounds to listen to when you fall asleep.

After you have the recordings, you can, of course, listen to them. But you have other options. Here are just a few possibilities:

- Email them to your friends or family. For instance, you can email a "letter" to your grandmother. You can send a birthday greeting from several of your friends to a friend who has moved away.
- Share your audio class notes with classmates who missed a class. Or share your audio notes in a group study session.

- Provide the audio for a slideshow or video presentation.
- Use the recordings as an alarm clock. (You learn more about setting alarms in Chapter 10, "Get Organized!")
- If you are really technologically advanced and have a digital video recorder, you can lay down your audio tracks for a digital movie.

Note

One of the newest uses of recordings is to create your own Internet radio broadcastings. This is known as *podcasting*. (You can use an iPod to do the recording, but you can also use other recorders, so the term *podcasting* can be a little misleading.) In addition to using the iPod, Apple is the creator of podcatcher software and publishes a podcast directory. Apple also provides a tutorial on how to create these broadcasts. You can learn more about podcasting in Chapter 6, "Music and More."

What You Need to Record

Sound like fun? Then let's gear up. To record, guess what you need? A recorder and a microphone. Ding! Ding! You're right. Let's take a look at the most popular products available.

Types of iPod Recorders

First up is Griffin's iTalk Voice Recorder (see Figure 7.1). You plug the recorder into the top of your iPod and record away. You can record up to 100 feet away, and this recorder includes a mini-speaker system so you can listen through the speaker, your headphones, or through iTunes (if you download your audio recordings to your computer). This product costs roughly $40, and you can purchase it at www.theistore.com or similar online sites.

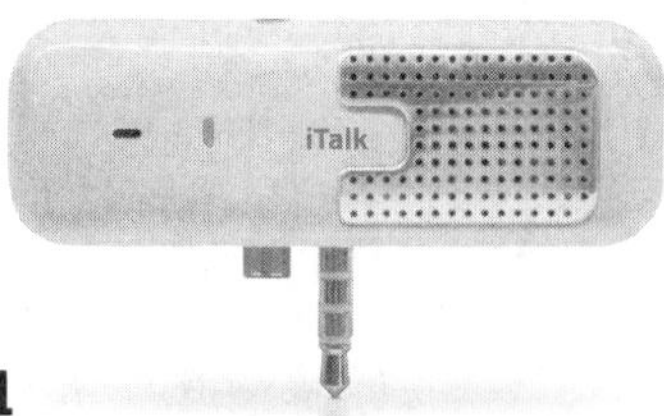

Figure 7.1

As the tag line for this product says, "You listen to your iPod every day. Now your iPod can listen to you."

Next up for consideration: DLO's VoiceNote Voice Recorder (see Figure 7.2) Priced the same as the iTalk, this product includes a lapel mic (a microphone that clips to your clothing) for recording, and you can adjust the recording level settings. Like the iTalk, you can play back the recordings through the built-in speaker system, through the iPod, or via iTunes (after downloading). Visit www.everythingipod.com for more information on this recorder.

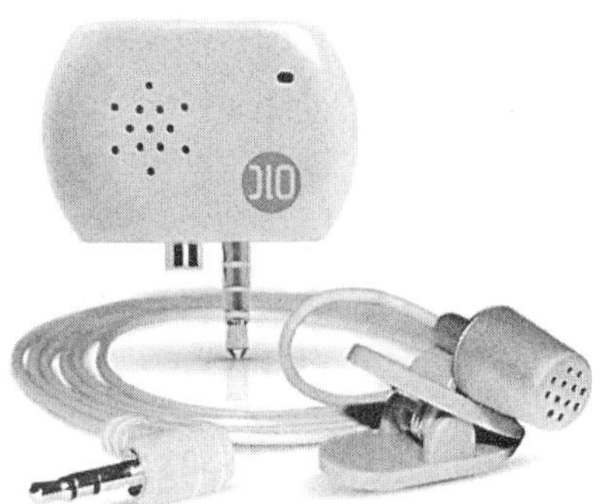

Figure 7.2

The DLO VoiceNote includes a built-in speaker and a lapel mic.

Caution

Currently, no recorders work for the iPod mini or iPod shuffle; these versions do not support recording devices.

Yet another choice is Belkin's iPod Voice Recorder ($60) and the Belkin Universal Mic Adapter for the iPod ($30), available at Belkin's site (http://catalog.belkin.com), www.everythingipod.com, or other online sites. The Universal Mic Adapter plugs into your iPod; you can then plug in any microphone with a 3.5mm plug and record. The iPod Voice Recorder product includes similar features as the iTalk and VoiceNote (see Figure 7.3).

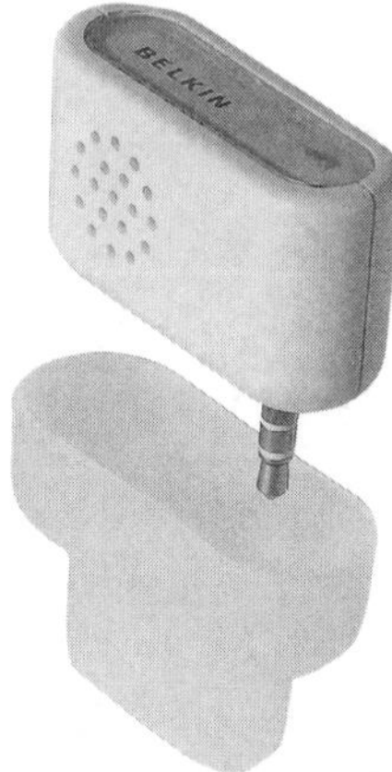

Figure 7.3

Belkin creates several iPod products, including a recorder.

iPod Recorders Versus Tape (or Other) Recorders

Now that you know the cost and the uses of a recorder, you might need some additional ammunition to convince your parents (or yourself). What are the benefits of the iPod recorder versus traditional recording devices? They boil down to these key points:

- **The amount of storage**—The typical tape recorder can store 60–120 minutes of talk time. Even flash memory types of recorders (available from Olympus and Sony, for instance), record at the most a few hours at a time. With the iPod, you can store literally thousands of hours of recordings.

- **Better organization for the recordings**—Because you don't have tapes to store, you can more easily store and organize your audio recordings. You can transfer them to iTunes, back them up to CDs, and edit them.

Coming Attractions

You can practice being the next big recording star using your iPod as a recorder. The recorder also has practical purposes for school, homework, and special assignments. The next chapter also includes the same mix of the fun and the practical. Here you see how you can listen to or even read books on your iPod.

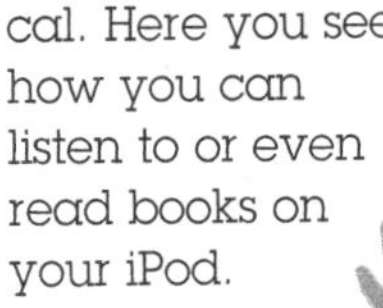

Chapter 8

Read All About It: iPod Books

Sometimes you aren't in the mood for music. Or maybe you are a book lover. Maybe you have to read a book for school. Perhaps you are going on a long trip. Listening to a book on your iPod provides just what you need in all of these instances. There are times when you might enjoy listening to books rather than reading them. Or the dramatic reading might be more suspenseful and interesting. Some people get carsick if they read in the car. You can see all the advantages of using your iPod as your own personal reader. This chapter covers all the various ways you can add audio books to your iPod experience.

Listening to Audio Books

You have several options for listening to books on your iPod. You can

- Purchase books designed for iPod (and other players), download them from the

Internet, and add them to your iPod, just like tunes. You can find audio books at iTunes.com, for instance.

- Rent books individually or sign up for a subscription service and get a certain number of books a month (much like NetFlix and some of the other video rental options). Audible.com, for instance, has a subscription plan.
- Borrow books from the library. Some libraries will download a book to your iPod. Others even let you borrow iPod shuffles with a book loaded.
- Transfer audio books from a CD to your computer. Then from the computer, add them to your iPod. Because iPod books are relatively new, there isn't much of a selection. (You can bet this will change soon.) CD audio book selections do offer more choices. Plus, you might even have some of these type of books already (listening to them on a long car ride, maybe?). And you can borrow audio books from the library as well.
- Create your own eBooks. An *eBook* is a text-version of a book you can read on special eBook readers. With a few tricks, you can create an eBook that you can read on your iPod via the Notes feature.

Note

iPod audio books are becoming so popular that one major bookseller (Waterstone) is adding kiosks inside its store for downloading books!

Listening to books on your iPod offers many other advantages, too. Just look at this list:

- The books are reasonably priced. Most audio books are priced similar to their print versions, and at iTunes, some books are offered at even lower prices. Some start at $2.95!
- You can listen to several books at once, and with the virtual bookmark feature, the iPod keeps track of your place in each book.
- Books on tape or CD require lots of physical storage space, you have to lug them around on trips, and they can become damaged. (For instance, suppose your new bulldog puppy Louie chews up the CD case and scratches the CD.) The iPod eliminates all of these worries (unless Louie gets hold of your iPod—yikes!).
- You are saving the environment (trees!).
- Love a book? You can listen to it again and again.
- Get immediate access to current books. You don't need to take a trip to the bookstore or library. Instead, download the title from an online bookseller as soon as it's available.

Sound cool? Then read on to see what options will work for you and your favorite mode of reading.

Buying and Downloading Books

The simplest way to listen to a book on your iPod is to purchase books designed for the iPod. (Note that other readers might work as well, but this isn't a book on all readers, just the *best*—your rockin' iPod. And some books might work *only* on the iPod.) Let's start with the simplest method of getting these books—from iTunes.

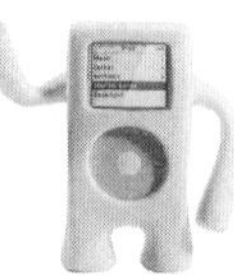

Tip

If you like to read comic books, check out the program Clickwheel. You can subscribe to and view Web comics on your Mac. Want to show a friend? Download your favorite ones to your iPod. A subscription costs $11.95, and you can get a shareware version of the program at www.apple.com/downloads/macosx/ipod_itunes/clickwheel.html

Getting Books from iTunes

One source for audio books is the same place you can buy your tunes. In addition to its vast music selection, the iTunes library includes more than 11,000 tiles (with more being added all the time). The Audiobook page (www.apple.com/itunes/store/books) lists the top books and details the bonuses on books for iTunes, including

- Something to meet everyone's favorite book type: thrillers to keep you on the edge of your seat, mysteries to keep you guessing, comedies to make you laugh, horror to keep you awake at night, love stories to make you dream of your Mr. (or Mrs.) Right, self-help books to improve yourself, and even educational titles to teach you something.

Tip

Audio books on languages (Spanish, Italian, French, and so on) are the perfect way to learn a new language. You might be taking a foreign language course in school (and if not now, you will be eventually), or you might just be interested in learning new languages (for your trips around the world!) Try an iPod book to help you master pronunciation.

- You can listen to 90 seconds of a title to see whether the book "sounds" interesting. You can hear what the book is about and also check whether the reading voice sounds cool.
- You can also download and listen to your favorite radio broadcasts, magazines, or newspapers to keep up to date on all the current news (such as whether your favorite movie stars will get married).

iTunes isn't your only source for books. You can also find titles at Audible.com, on publisher's websites, and on eBay.

Tip

Some sites specialize in books whose copyright has expired. So if you have to read any classic works for school, check these sites because you might find a free downloadable version. Try AudioBooksForFree.com.

To purchase a title, follow the online instructions for that particular site. For instance, purchasing a title at Audible.com works like purchasing a title at Amazon.com: You add a book to your shopping cart and then check out. It appears in your personal online library, and you can then download it to your computer. From there, you import into iTunes and then sync your iPod, adding the book. Note that if you use a PC, you need to use Audible.com's AudibleManager, a software program that manages the download process.

To protect the rights of the authors, the audio files are stored in a special encrypted format. You cannot convert them to MP3 files, and the special format doesn't work on all portable players.

Tip

For some titles at Audible.com, you can also burn the audio book to a CD and listen to it on a CD player. The book description includes this information if this option is available for that particular title.

Subscribing to a Book Service

If you read a lot, you might consider a different method of getting books—through a subscription service. One of the most popular is Audible.com. (You can also purchase individual books from this site, as described in the previous section.) When you visit the site, you have to register as a user to get access to its online catalog. Audible.com has more than 27,000 books, newspapers, and magazines.

You have several options for finding titles of interest. You can search for titles, browse directories, read customer reviews, and listen to samples of books.

Tip

In addition to downloading the audio book to your iPod, you can also listen to streaming audio on your computer. (You have to stay connected to the Internet.) You can also download the book and listen to it from your computer later (you don't have to be connected to the Internet to listen).

Audible.com's special AudibleListener monthly membership plan allows you to download a certain number of books each month. The site offers several levels of membership including the BasicListener (one book plus one magazine, newspaper, or radio program for $14.95) to PremiumListener (two books per month for $21.95).

Borrowing Books from the Library

For the budget-minded, your library might provide a free source of audio books. Often your library has only cassette or CD versions of the book, but some libraries will put a book on your iPod. And some even will let you borrow a player (the iPod shuffle) with a book preloaded! Check with your local library to see what's available.

Note

Expect services to expand also. It might not be too far into the future where *every* library lets users browse and download books. A new service available now, OverDrive, lets library patrons download eBooks and digital audio books online. Visit www.overdrive.com to see a list of participating libraries.

Adding CD Audio Books to Your iPod

Book collections specific to iPod and other similar players aren't as comprehensive as other sources such as print and CD-based books. You can use your iPod to listen to any CD-based books that you have. The process works *somewhat* like ripping music CDs. You add the audio book from the CD to iTunes and then sync iTunes with your iPod to transfer the files to your iPod. You do need to make some changes to how you import the audio content. Check Apple's online help or search for this topic to find specific instructions.

Sources for CD books are many; all major book retailers offer a wide range of audio books. You can also purchase these books online. To save money, you might also look into used audio books at retail stores, such as Half-Price Books, and online sites, such as eBay, Half.com, and the used listings on Amazon.com.

You can also rent books at sites such as Audio-To-Go (www.audiotogo.com) and Booksfree.com. You select your book wish list, and they mail you books as they become available. Shipping is free, and they provide a mailing label for returns.

Creating eBooks to Read on Your iPod

If you don't like to listen, you can still use your iPod to read books. You can find accessories that let you convert text or eBooks (which you can find online) into a format you can read on your iPod (through the Notes feature). You upload the book and the program makes the text iPod-friendly.

Try Book2Pod for Mac users, available at www.tomsci.com/book2pod/ or www.apple.com/downloads/macosx/ipod_itunes/book2pod.html, and iPodLibrary for Windows users, available at http://sturm.t35.com/ipodlibrary.

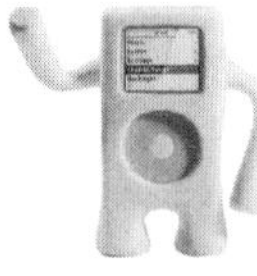

Tip

You can find eBooks for purchase and free (to encourage you to purchase more later). Sites include www.free-ebooks.net, www.ebooks.com, www.gutenberg.org, and others.

You can also get copies of important documents in a format you can read using your iPod. For instance, get a copy of the Constitution of the United States. This utility is called iCon, and you can find it at www.apple.com/downloads/macosx/ipod_itunes/icon.html. For the spiritual-minded, get a freeware copy of the Bible (plus features such as daily proverbs). This program, called BiblePlayer, is also available at Apple's site www.apple.com/downloads/macosx/ipod_itunes/bibleplayer.html.

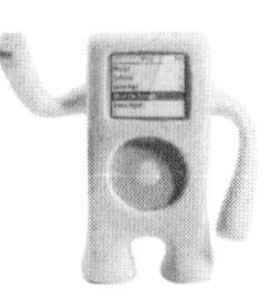

Tip

Check the system requirements for utility programs from www.apple.com/downloads/macosx. Some work only with the Mac; others work both with the Mac and Windows-based PCs.

Coming Attractions

Reading is fun (well, for some people). What other fun can you have with your iPod beyond music? How about games? That's the topic of the next chapter.

Chapter 9

Playing Games

Your iPod comes loaded with some games to waste away the time, uh, I mean, improve your hand-eye coordination. You can play Brick, Music Quiz, Parachute, or Solitaire. If you are totally into games, though, these aren't going to satisfy your twitching fingers. Instead, you might look for other games that you can add to your iPod (and add your own soundtrack by listening to music and playing).

Currently, most games are text-based, explorer-type games. You read the story and then select what you want to do. Read the postcard? Ignore the postcard? Follow the advice on the postcard? What you choose affects what happens next. You role-play as a character, trying to achieve the goal of the game (rescue a kingdom, solve a mystery, and so on).

With Apple's plans to update all new iPods with a color screen and Apple's request for iPod game programmers, expect the game situation to improve. Right now, your choices aren't that varied, but you can find some interesting text stories.

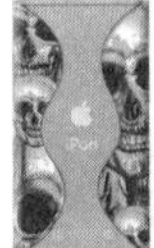

Caution
Check with your parents about these games and their story lines. Depending on your age, some might not be appropriate.

What Games Are Available?

The first company to offer iPod games (beyond the Apple-supplied games) is Malinche Entertainment (www.malinche.net). You can download these games to your iPod or iPod shuffle. These games focus on interactive story lines and cost $9.95. Because the iPod doesn't include a keyboard, you select actions or options using the click wheel.

Caution
Not all iPod generations work with these games. If you have questions, email Malinche. They include a link about versions on their website.

You can get a description of current and upcoming titles; current titles include

- The First Mile, a horror story. Fight to stay alive and get out of this backwater town, Dead Rock, Arkansas. Expect to meet ghosts, demons, monsters, and helpful and unhelpful characters on your path.

- Greystone, a murder mystery. You are the detective, and you are challenged to solve this murder mystery as an undercover patient at Greystone.
- Pentari: First Light, a fantasy adventure. Wizards have taken over the city of Delphin, and you are charged with reclaiming the city. The game description claims "You have nearly 300 rooms to explore including a city to be searched, an underground complex to explore, as well as monsters and wizards to contend with." Are you ready for the challenge?

XOPlay also produces iPod games based on several story lines such as a knight battling enemies. You can find information about their games at the website (www.xoplay.com).

You can find another source of stories (and a program for creating your own stories, covered next) at www.ipodsoft.com. You can be a fat Ninja named Play-Dough; pretend like you are Napoleon Dynamite in a game of the same name; be a crime-scene investigator (CSI Man); make choices about taking care of your braces (The Orthadontist [who misspelled that one?]); try to overthrow the king (Peasant Quest); participate in the Legend of the Corned Beef Muchachos; play rock, paper, scissors; survive a day in middle school (Survive Pioneer Middle School); be a detective (Detective Harrison); enjoy life as an ant (Ant Life); play Tic Tac Toe; test your trivia of

Aqua Teen Hunger Force; solve riddles; take a stick man on an adventure; and more.

Use the links at the ipodsoft.com site to download the games and then add them to your iPod.

Creating Your Own Games

If you like to tell your own stories, you can create your own games with iStory Creator. The program doesn't require programming ability and claims you need no HTML coding experience to create a game, but if you don't even know what HTML is (it's a language used to design and program web pages), you might need some help. It might be a good project to work on with an older sibling, parent, or even as a class assignment.

In any case, you basically create a story with options, and the option the player selects determines the outcome of the story. You might, for instance, create your own version of Little Red Riding Hood. What if she decided to have a picnic with her friends and eat the food? What if she lost her cape and went to find it? Use a common story to start, and then as you gain experience, you can tell your own tales with funny, scaring, or thrilling endings. You can also check out some of the stories at ipodsoft.com to get some ideas as well.

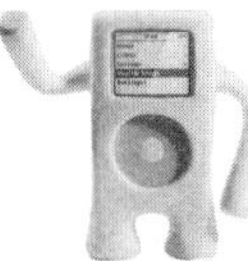

Tip

You can also create reference material and quizzes with this software.

You can download iStory Creator at www.ipodsoft.com. The website also includes instructions for downloading the program to your iPod.

Coming Attractions

In addition to having fun with your iPod, you can also use it to keep organized; keep to-do lists of homework; and manage your list of friends, family, classmates, teachers, and others with your iPod. Set an alarm clock to wake you up in the morning—not with a loud beeping, but with your own personal play list. You can also go to sleep listening to your music with a sleep timer. The next chapter covers these iPod options for making your life super-organized.

Chapter 10

Get Organized!

Your parents might complain that the iPod is simply for entertainment and doesn't really have anything useful, but ah, it does. It can replace your mom coming in your room at the crack of dawn telling you its time to get up. It can also remind you to call home or be home at your curfew time, which will make your parents very happy.

In addition to the alarm features, you can also keep contact information so you have handy phone numbers and addresses of friends, family, and classmates. Want more useful organization features? You can make sure you keep all of your appointments (homework assignments, orthodontist appointments, and so on) and notes.

iPod includes several organization features: Clock, Contacts, Calendar, and Notes. The first part of this chapter looks at the features your iPod has but you might not know about. Then you explore some accessory programs to supercharge these tools, making them even more useful.

What Comes on Your iPod

As mentioned, your iPod already includes some organizational tools, which you can find in the Extras menu. Here's a quick summary of what you can do with these features:

- With the Clock feature, you can set an alarm, a sleep timer, and also view (and change) the date and time (see Figure 10.1).

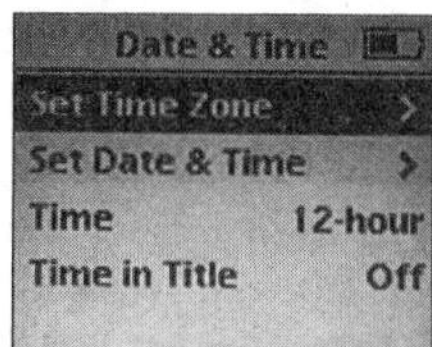

Figure 10.1

iPod's clock feature lets you set the date, time zone, and alarms.

Note

Your iPod automatically adjusts the time if you change to a different time zone. Pretty cool!

Caution

Make sure the date and time is correct if you rely on an iPod alarm. Also, consider plugging it into a power outlet so it doesn't run out of power (if you listen to it while going to sleep and don't use the sleep feature to automatically power it off).

- You can add contact information from contact programs such as Microsoft Outlook, Microsoft Outlook Express, and Palm Desktop. As the Apple site says, "Little black address books are so last millennium." To keep contacts on your iPod, the iPod menu includes a helpful set of instructions and sample.

Tip

All of the contact programs compatible with iPod enable you to save your contact information in a virtual business card or *vcard*. You have to save your contacts as this type of card, enable iPod to function as a disk (covered in Chapter 11, "Storing Data and Pictures on Your iPod"), and then copy the vcards to your iPod. (The vcard format is recognized by Microsoft Outlook and Apple's Mail program as well.)

- Need to check the date? Or want to schedule appointments (and reminders) using your iPod? Check out the Calendar feature (see Figure 10.2).
- If you set up your iPod to work as a disk (the topic of the next chapter), you can add notes (see Figure 10.3). And more fun than notes, you can also download web content such as directions, movie times, and reviews. You learn more about some of these options later in this chapter.

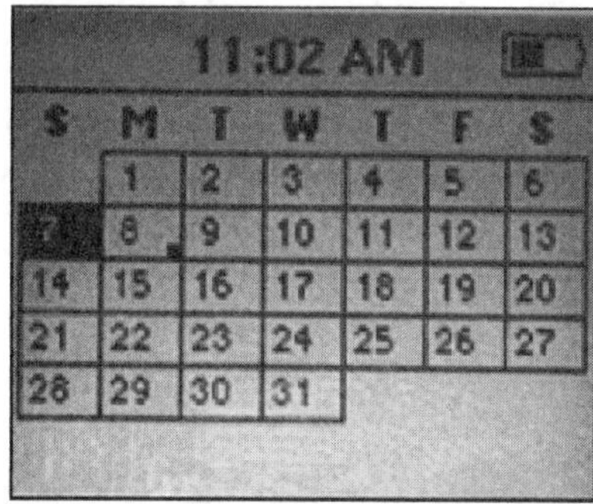

Figure 10.2

With the calendar feature you can make sure you're always at the right place at the right time.

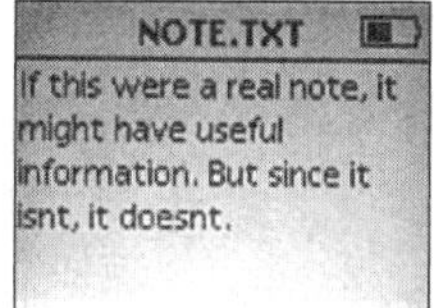

Figure 10.3

Taking your notes to school has never been so easy!

Waking Up on Time (and Falling Asleep to Music)

The iPod alarm clock is okay, but if you want something more like a "regular" alarm clock or if you want extra features such as snooze, you might investigate some add-ons. You can select from two types of alarm add-ons: a program you run on the iPod or an alarm clock dock for your iPod. Which one rings your bell?

iPod Utilities

Several programs are available that have the same features as the iPod alarm and sleep feature, plus more. Many of these programs are shareware or freeware, so they are worth checking out because the cost is little or nothing. You can find two such programs at the download page at Apple.com (www.apple.com/downloads/macosx/ipod_itunes/): iRooster and iSleep.

iRooster lets you create alarm clocks, and you can select to wake up to a special playlist, songs from your entire library, or a random playlist (created by iRooster). You can also hit the snooze for just "five more minutes!" iRooster also includes Lullabye so you can fall asleep listening to music of your choice. (This utility works only on Mac systems.)

iSleep offers similar features as iRooster; it includes a snooze mode, a sleep feature, and an alarm clock (see Figure 10.4). This program also works with iTunes and DVD Player.

Caution

Although several of the programs described in this chapter are available at Apple's site, Apple includes a disclaimer,

so read the fine print. Basically, Apple doesn't provide help if you have questions with the program, and they don't guarantee these programs work as described. You have to test them out yourself.

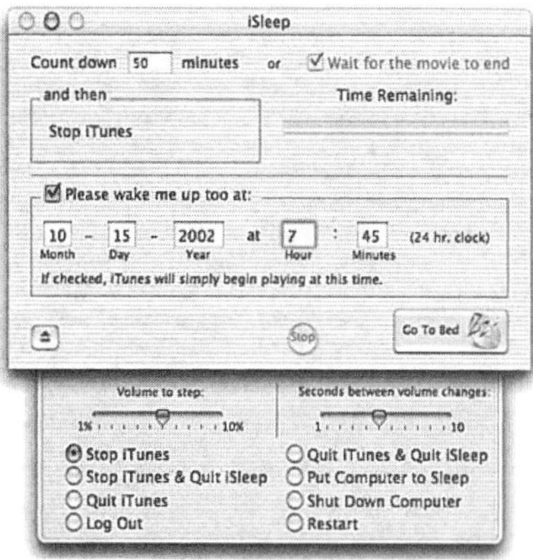

Figure 10.4

Set an alarm clock and sleep features using iSleep.

iPod Alarm Clock Docks

In addition to utilities you can add to your iPod, you can also purchase alarm clock docks. These combine several features into one module: AM/FM radio, a dock that recharges your iPod, regular and iPod alarms, a digital clock, and speakers for playing radio or iPod music.

For instance, the iHome system includes a dock that will work with the iPod and iPod mini. It automatically sets the alarm for the same time the next day, saving you the trouble. Also, if you use the sleep feature, the sound volume gradually decreases as your beddy-bye time winds down.

Hammacher Schlemmer (www.hammacher.com) offers a similar product. You can listen to your music library through the iPod and the dock speakers, and you can wake up to a song, buzzer, or radio. The price is roughly $100, but remember if you purchase this unit, you won't necessarily need a dock, a charger, or a speaker system.

Scheduling a Tune List

As mentioned previously, you can download your schedule from a calendar program such as iCal and then have it handy. With the special iCal Calling iTunes! utility, you can combine scheduling with a playlist (for Mac only). For instance, what songs sound good for lunchtime? Schedule a particular playlist to play at noon. What about that bewitching hour right before bedtime? What songs will rock you to sleep? You can schedule lists for any time throughout the day. You can get this shareware program at www.apple.com/downloads/macosx/

ipod_itunes/icalcallingitunes.html. (You need the program iCal for this utility to work.)

Keeping Track of Friends and Notes

iPod's built-in Contacts and Notes feature are pretty basic. What if you want more muscle? More features? What if you want it all on your iPod, without having to use your computer and *then* download the stuff to your iPod? Then check out some of the programs designed to make adding contacts and keeping notes easier.

One program, iPodCopy, includes music features as well as a contact manager that lets you add, view, and delete contacts and synchronize your contacts with Microsoft Outlook. With its notes feature, you can create, edit, view, and delete notes right on your iPod. You can also sync with Outlook. For a complete list of what this program offers, visit www.ipodcopy.com. You can demo a version, and if you like it, pay the $15 fee to get the full-fledged program.

A similar shareware program is also available at www.apple.com/downloads/macosx/ ipod_itunes/ipodit.html. In addition to enabling you to transfer PIM data (personal information manager—computer makers *love* acronyms), you can download weather forecasts and news headlines with iPod It (see Figure 10.5).

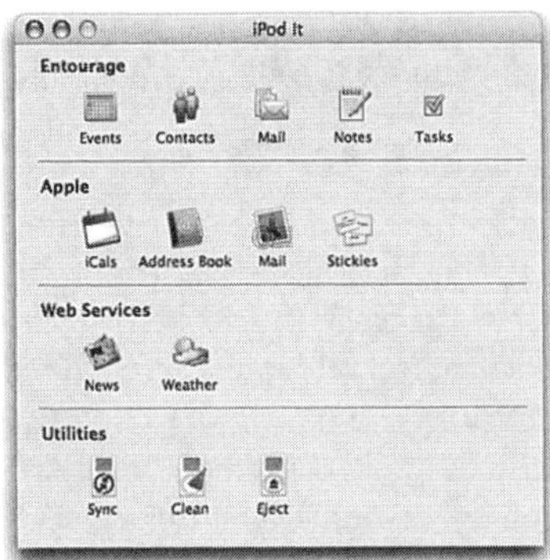

Figure 10.5

See how iPod It adds more organization to your iPod and your life.

What if you just want to be able to add notes without the hassle of using your computer? After all, your computer isn't always handy, but your iPod usually is. In that case, use iPlod to write messages, store phone numbers, create to-do lists, and record web addresses. The site for this freeware utility is www.apple.com/downloads/macosx/ipod_itunes/iplod.html.

Tip

Here's another cool thing: Convert your email into audio tracks so you can listen to your email from iTunes on your computer or on your iPod. Try the demo version from www.apple.com/downloads/macosx/ipod_itunes/earmail.html.

Cool Content for On the Go

You can look up lots of info on the Internet: movie reviews, driving directions (so your parents know how to drive you to birthday parties and friends' homes), and more. What if you want these to appear on your iPod? Well, you need to find a utility program to complement your iPod and make you the go-to-girl (or guy) for the latest on weather, news, and other stuff.

Note

Are you thinking, "Why do I care about the weather?" What if you are going to an outdoor event? You need to know what to wear. And keeping up on latest news can help with social studies and history classes. So before you think "fuddy-duddy," think how this information can make your decisions and school work easier.

For driving directions from MapQuest, MapBlast, or Google Maps, check out PodQuest. You can download the directions from these sites to your iPod so you have them handy when you are in the car. This shareware program is available at www.apple.com/downloads/macosx/ipod_itunes/podquest.html.

For information about movie times in your particular area, try MoviesToGo. You enter your zip code and then download the shows, times, and addresses of theaters in that area. The site for this shareware program is www.apple.com/downloads/macosx/ipod_itunes/moviestogo.html.

Coming Attractions

A music player. An organizer. An alarm clock. What more can you do with your iPod? You can also use it to store and share files such as pictures. (Setting up the iPod as a disk is also needed for adding notes and other features described in this book.) The next chapter covers how to use your iPod to store and share files.

Chapter 11

Storing Data and Pictures on Your iPod

You can use any iPod model (except the shuffle) to store and display pictures as well as other files. How might this come in handy in your busy life? Here are just a few scenarios to think about:

- You could create a photo album of your new puppy (or friends, vacation, boyfriends, and so on), store it on your iPod, and show all your friends.
- If you have a digital camera and are running out of storage room, move your pictures to your iPod to free up storage space.
- Create a digital photo show with sound and play your little musical on your TV through your iPod.

- Use your iPod to store photography for a class project, school newspaper, or yearbook.
- Suppose that you are working on a report on the computer at school and need to also do some work at home. Transfer the file to your iPod and take it with you.
- Use your iPod and its picture-storing features to create a presentation. No more boring book reports or science exhibits for you.

This chapter looks at all the possibilities of the iPod as a photo album and hard drive.

Storing Photos

You can store up to 25,000 photos on your iPod. If you have a photo-editing program (such as iPhoto for the Mac, Adobe Photoshop Elements, or Adobe Album for Windows), you can transfer pix directly from your camera to your photo library and then to your iPod. Or if you have a special connector, you can transfer photos directly from your camera to your iPod. (This camera connector is covered later in this section.)

With the new color screens, you can display 25 full-color thumbnails (mini pictures) at a time on your iPod. Just like you can scroll through songs, you can scroll through pictures using the click wheel. To see a larger version of a picture, simply click the Select button (the center button) and there's your photo. It's like a photo album but without the hassle of those plastic inserts and printed pictures!

Using a Camera Connector

If you want the convenience of being able to move photos directly from a camera to your iPod, consider investing in an iPod Camera Connector (see Figure 11.1). This tool is reasonably priced ($29), and you can move pictures from the camera directly to the iPod.

Because you are freeing up camera space, the iPod Camera Connector also lets you take many more pictures than you could with a digital camera, even one with extra storage.

Figure 11.1

Use a camera dock to move photos directly from your camera to your iPod.

The connector works like this: The iPod plugs into the dock connector, and then your camera's USB cable plugs into the dock. Your pictures are then transferred. You can read reviews and get more information about this device at http://store.apple.com.

Another option for transferring photos to your iPod is Belkin's Media Reader for iPod with Dock Connector (see Figure 11.2). It uses a FireWire connector to transfer digital photos very quickly. You can insert any one of the six supported media cards including CompactFlash (Types 1 and 2), SmartMedia, Secure Digital (SD), Memory Stick, and Multimedia Card (MMC) directly into the device and then directly to your iPod. You can get more information about this product including price (around $50) at http://catalog.belkin.com.

Figure 11.2

Use this media reader to transfer images from camera cards to your iPod.

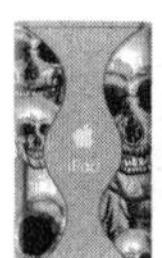

Caution

One drawback that reviewers note about the reader is that it uploads pictures using a film roll metaphor. That's okay if you

have one set of pictures, but if you transfer many images to your iPod, they are all placed in one big film roll. You'll have to sort through and separate them into albums in your photo program. The Belkin Media Reader does not work with the iPod mini or iPod shuffle.

Creating a Musical Slideshow

In addition to viewing your pictures on the iPod, you can also display your images for everyone to see. You can, of course, simply hand your iPod to someone and show them your pictures using this display. Or you can create a slideshow of pictures and display them using several options. One option is using pictures and music on your computer to create a slideshow. For instance, iPhoto (a Mac program) and Adobe Photoshop Elements 4 (for Windows) include slideshow features. You can then view the slideshow on your computer.

As another option, you can connect your iPod to a TV or projector and then use it to display your photos (and play your music). To do so, you need a special AV cable. Apple sells an iPod AV cable (compatible only with the color iPod) that you can use to connect to your TV and view photo slide-shows with music on your TV. The cost is around $19; check out http://store.apple.com for information on this product.

If you want connections for the TV as well as other equipment (such as your PowerBook and iMovie or Apple DVD player), look into the Monster iTV Link ($40), available at www.monstercable.com or through Apple's store (http://store.apple.com). This connector uses the highest quality video and audio cable technology.

You can also create and store PowerPoint presentations on your iPod and use your iPod (instead of a laptop) to hook up to a TV or projector. This process takes a few extra steps; you have to export the PowerPoint slides in the JPEG format, import them to the iPod using iTunes, and then add music.

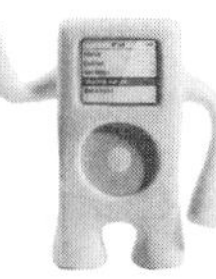

Tip

Although you probably don't do many PowerPoint presentations now, you might as you continue in school, so just keep this thought in the back of your head. Also, your parents might be interested in this feature if they have to do slide presentations in their work.

If you don't want to manually create the presentation, you can use a utility program to help with the process. With ZappTek's iPresent It ($17.95), you can convert PowerPoint, PDF, and Keynote (a presentation software for the Mac) presentations into slideshows. You can find more about this product at www.zapptek.com/ipresent-it/.

Storing Data

In addition to storing photos, your iPod is also a versatile storage unit for other files, such as your World History report or creative writing assignment, that you create in a word processing program (such as Microsoft Word). Using your iPod as a storage device is much better than a disk or even a CD.

To add files to your iPod, all you need to do is to set up your iPod as a storage device. You can do so by following these steps:

1. If you don't see your iPod on your desktop and if iTunes starts automatically when you plug in your iPod, select your iPod in the Source column on the left side of the iTunes window. When you do so, two new buttons appear in the bottom-right corner of the iTunes window.
2. Click the first button from the left (see Figure 11.3). You should see the iPod Preferences dialog box.
3. Make sure the iPod tab is selected and then within that window, click the General tab (see Figure 11.4).

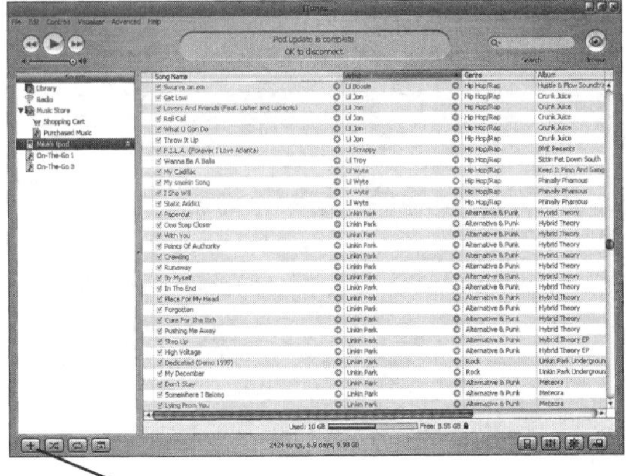

Figure 11.3

Use the first button from the left to display iPod options.

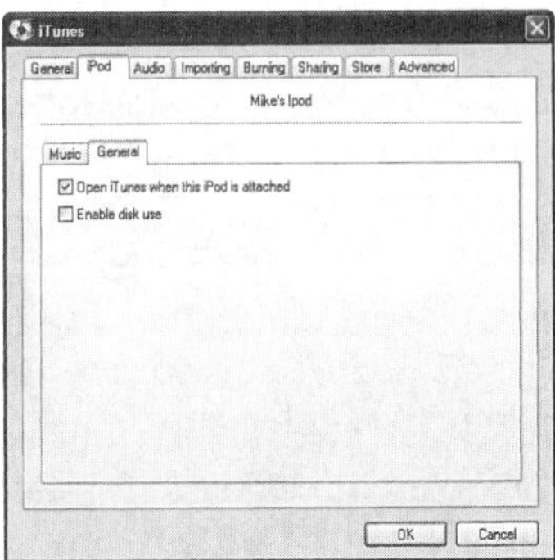

Figure 11.4

Use this dialog box to turn on the storage capabilities of the iPod.

4. Check Enable Disk Use and click OK.

Now you can open and view files on your iPod just as if it were a drive. You can drag and drop files to the iPod and vice versa (from the iPod to your computer). Neat, huh!

Coming Attractions

Well, you've just about heard all the cool things you can do with the iPod. Remember, though, that the iPod is a hot product, so new gadgets will appear all the time. Keep up on what's new by visiting Apple's site or your local Apple store.

What's left to mention? Taking good care of your precious music player, book reader, recorder, stereo system, language translator, hard disk, photo album...you get the picture. The next chapter covers maintaining what's probably become a central part of your life, your beloved iPod.

Chapter 12

Maintain It: Chargers, Batteries, and Clean Up

Let's be upfront about this chapter: The gadgets covered aren't the most fun accessories. But think of it this way. If these accessories can keep your music playing longer and keep your iPod smooth and sleek, it's worth reading about some of the less exciting accessories. Here you'll find information about chargers, battery packs, and cleaning supplies.

Charge It Up

Your iPod came with a charger, and you can use this to keep your iPod always ready to belt out a tune. But you might consider adding other chargers. You can buy replacement chargers, docks that charge (covered in Chapter 5, "Hangin' at Your Crib: iPod Docks and Remotes"), and car chargers (featured in Chapter 3, "Take It with You: iPod Travel Accessories"). Here let's look at some of the special types of chargers and battery options:

- **DLO Charge n' Sync Retractable Cable Kit**—This kit includes a little bit of everything: cables for connecting to your computer, a power adapter for charging, and a dock connector. All this for the price of roughly $40, available at www.dlo.com and www.everythingipod.com.

Tip

You can find a list of other battery packs (including car chargers) at www.wirelessgalaxy.com.

- **myPower Battery Pack for iPod**—When you plug your iPod into this dock, it runs off batteries, giving you anywhere from 20 to 42 hours of additional play (depending on your iPod model). Note that the extra playtime is expensive; this battery pack runs $85 or so, available at www.everythingipod.com.
- **Belkin Backup Battery Pack**—Similar to the preceding battery pack, this pack lets you run your iPod on batteries (4 AA batteries). For the price of $50–$60, you can expect to get up to 15 hours of music playtime running on this battery supply. Visit www.theistore.com for information on this product.
- **TunePower Rechargeable Battery Pack**—Also made by Belkin, this pack adds about 8–10 hours of battery-powered play. The difference

is that you can recharge the TunePower *and* your iPod with the AC wall charger. And this pack works with all iPod and iPod minis. It's pricey ($99), but you don't have the added cost of batteries. For all the specs on this product, go to thinkdifferentstore.com.

- **TuneJuice**—If you want just a little more playing time, consider the compact TuneJuice that adds up to four hours of playtime and is powered by a 9-volt battery.
- **Solio Solar Charger**—And what about those outdoorsy camper types? Or those concerned about the environment? This charger sets up like a small tripod and gets its energy from the sun. Plug in your iPod and get a full charge in about two hours. It costs about $100.

Caution

If you use the solar charger, you are at the mercy of mother nature; it must be sunny for the charger to work!

Cleaning Your iPod

Your iPod can get dirty. Fingerprints. Dust. Ketchup. Scratches. You shouldn't use any old household product to clean it up. Instead, you can buy cleaning material designed for the sensitive surface of your precious iPod.

Tip

One way to help keep your iPod clean is to purchase some type of cover or case. Chapter 4, "Stylin' and Profilin': iPod Skins, Tattoos, Cases, and More," provides information on *lots* of options.

The iKlear Cleaning Kit is Apple's recommended cleaner, and the kit comes with a cleaner, chamois polishing cloth, and travel size cleaning supplies (a cute little small chamois cloth and Wet/Dry wipes). What makes this $19.95 product so special? The company sites several things. First, the award-winning formula is anti-static, non-toxic, non-damaging, alcohol-free, and ammonia-free. (Maybe it's just water! Just kidding!) Second, the cleaner also leaves an anti-static coating that helps reduce wear and fingerprints. You can purchase iKlear at places that sell iPod products, as well as online at sites such as www.theistore.com.

Note

You can also use the cleaning kit to clean up your Mac computer or PowerBook.

If fingerprints aren't the problem, you can buy polishers that help remove the scratches. The iCleaner Pro kit comes with a polishing glove and polish that will "put the shine back on your iPod now!" Purchase the product for roughly $20 at online sites such as www.everythingipod.com.

A similar product for removing scratches is Ice Créme M Scratch Remover. You get two products: one for removing scratches from acrylic and plastic surfaces and one for polishing and removing scratches from metal. The kit also includes application and polishing cloths. For this particular cleaning kit, expect to pay $25 or so (available at www.thinkdifferentstore.com).

Coming Attractions

Well, throughout this book, you should have read about enough accessories to fill your Christmas and birthday lists for years to come. Keep in mind, though, that new iPod versions are introduced regularly as are new products for your iPod.

What can you expect to see? Bigger iPods (in terms of storage) and possibly small iPods (in terms of size). Color displays as standard. Cell phones that also play music, possibly even an iPod cell phone. More integration with storing all types of media. More games and other functions for the player, including a new video iPod for playing videos. Check out your local Apple store or visit Apple's website to keep up-to-date on what's coming next. And don't forget to start saving your allowance, babysitting money, change, or other cash sources.